W9-ASL-712

THE
PERFECT
POTATO

THE
PERFECT
POTATO

Over 100 Fabulous Recipes
—from Appetizers to Desserts—
for Potato Lovers Everywhere

DIANE SIMONE VEZZA

VILLARD
BOOKS

A Running Heads Book

Copyright © 1993 by Running Heads Incorporated

All rights reserved under International and Pan-American Copyright
Conventions. Published in the United States by Villard Books, a division
of Random House, Inc., New York, and simultaneously in Canada by
Random House of Canada Limited, Toronto.

Villard Books is a registered trademark of Random House, Inc.

Library of Congress Cataloging-in-Publication Data
Vezza, Diane Simone.
The perfect potato / Diane Simone Vezza ; illustrations
by Arlene Cooper.
p.   cm.
Includes index.
ISBN 0-679-74580-7
1. Cookery (Potatoes)   I. Cooper, Arlene.   II. Title.
TX803.P8D58   1992
841.6'521—dc20   92-16738
CIP

THE PERFECT POTATO
was conceived and produced by
Running Heads Incorporated
55 West 21 Street
New York, NY 10010

Creative Director: Linda Winters
Editor: Rose K. Phillips   Designer: Helene Berinsky
Managing Editor: Jill Hamilton   Production Associate: Belinda Hellinger

Illustrations by Arlene Cooper

Typeset by Trufont Typographers Inc.
Color separations by Hong Kong Scanner Craft Company, Ltd.
Printed and bound in Singapore by Tien Wah Press (Pte.) Ltd.

9 8 7 6 5 4 3 2
First Edition

This book is affectionately dedicated to my husband Jerry,
who can still look a potato in the eye and eat it.

ACKNOWLEDGMENTS

Thanks to Marta Hallett at Running Heads for believing in me and to my editor at Villard, Emily Bestler, for her guidance. Also thanks to Rose K. Phillips, Tom Fiffer, and Jill Hamilton for their enthusiasm and support.

On the home front, thanks to my family . . . Anne, Paul, Pat, Tracy, Rob, Landi, and Kira for "suffering" through various stages of tasting and giving me encouragement and love.

Special thanks to the friends and family that have openly shared their kitchens, recipes, and tables, especially Terry Cohen who shared her favorite potato knish recipe with me (and you).

And finally, love and gratitude to my other half. Without his inspiration none of this would have been possible.

CONTENTS

INTRODUCTION

The raw potato is an unlikely object of veneration: Irregular in form and covered with the dust of the earth from which it was plucked, the average potato looks as unprepossessing as a stone. But subject it to the right amount of heat, and the lowly potato is transformed into something of a culinary wonder. What could be more appealing, after all, than a simple baked spud, popped open and emitting a cloud of fragrant steam? What speaks more eloquently of home and hearth than a bowl of buttery mashed potatoes? And is there anything more addictive than an ethereal batch of *pommes frites*? No wonder that the potato is the world's largest vegetable crop: Over 290 million tons are harvested each year in more than 130 countries. The average American consumes 125 pounds of potatoes annually, while his European cousin puts away nearly twice that amount. As a crop, the potato is a model of agricultural efficiency: An acre of potatoes yields as much food as two acres of grain, and does so in less time. And the average potato is nutrient dense—high in vitamins, minerals, and dietary fiber, cholesterol-free, and extremely low in fat and sodium.

Still, until very recently, most people looked on the potato as essentially humble: tasty, yes, but prosaic, the culinary equivalent of a sensible pair of shoes. Lucky for us aficionados, all that is changing. Over the past decade the potato has experienced an incredible renaissance. "Homely" mashed potatoes suddenly began appearing on the menus of the world's most elegant restaurants, from Lutèce in New York to Paris's Jamin. Imaginative chefs, inspired by the potato's versatility, took it from the realm of the side dish and used it as the base for a panoply of extraordinary soups, salads, breads, hors d'oeuvres, and entrées. And farmers and greengrocers, taking note of this rising interest, introduced a host of new varieties in a rainbow of colors, from rosy pink to golden yellow to an astonishing deep purple. We have finally begun to give the potato its due. But lest we congratulate ourselves too heartily, it's worthwhile to note that long before the first potato and goat cheese pizza appeared in the dreams of some inspired California chef, another group of potato lovers were reaping the benefits of its diversity and adaptability.

POTATOES PAST: HISTORY

Some five thousand years ago, the Incas of South America made one of the most significant discoveries in culinary history. No one knows what inspired them to begin harvesting the wild plant now known as *Solanum tuberosum*, or what gastronomic epiphany led them to eschew the green leaves in favor of the gnarled root ball below, but contemporary cooks owe them a tremendous debt of gratitude. Eight thousand feet above sea level, the Incas were able to grow a dazzling variety of the precious tubers, in colors ranging from white, orange, and pink to purple, blue, green, brown, and even black. The Andean potatoes could be as small and slender as a child's finger or as round and robust as a grapefruit. Undoubtedly, the range of flavors and textures was equally great. To this day, no group of people has been more enthusiastic about potatoes than the Incas, for whom they actually became objects of worship.

As with all the riches of the New World, it was inevitable that the potato would make its way into European hands, on both sides of the Atlantic. Culinary historians alternately credit Francisco Pizarro and Sir Francis Drake for introducing the potato to Europe and North America, but it is Sir Walter Raleigh who became its most ardent champion, planting it on his estate in England and even presenting several plants to his patron, Elizabeth I. Alas, her chef, making an understandable error, served the bitter leaves instead of the root, thereby singlehandedly consigning the vegetable to obscurity for several centuries.

It was in the 1700s that the potato experienced its first renaissance, notably in Prussia and France, where King Frederick William I and the French pharmacist Antoine-Auguste Parmentier touted it as the answer to widespread hunger. One hundred years later, the rest of Europe caught on, but nowhere more so than in Ireland, where abundant rainfall and boggy soil combined to produce an ideal climate for potatoes. We can thank the Irish for the word *spud*, Gaelic for the spade that dug them from the earth. The Irish became so dependent on this versatile vegetable that the famous potato blight of the 1840s resulted in over one million deaths by starvation.

POTATOES PERFECT: NUTRITION

Today's potatoes are not only more resistant to disease than their nineteenth-century counterparts, but they are also on the way to something approaching nutritional perfection, as genetic engineers work to develop a potato with a higher-quality protein than that in beef. Even in its present state, the potato is a nutritional bonanza. One medium cooked potato is exceptionally high in fiber and low in calories—at 110, fewer than an apple of the same size. It offers 50 percent of the recommended daily allowance for vitamin C, 15 percent for vitamin B^6, 8 percent for iron, thiamin, and folacin, and over 100 percent of the RDA for vitamin K. In addition, potatoes contain roughly 800 milligrams of potassium—more than an average serving of virtually any other food, and enough, medical research suggests, to reduce significantly or even eliminate the risk of stroke.

With only 40 more calories than white potatoes of the same size, sweet potatoes are equally nutrient-rich, with nearly twice the RDA for vitamin A, 33 percent for vitamin C, and an abundant supply of potassium, calcium, iron, and niacin. Of course, the addition of fats—in the form of butter, cream, or oil for deep frying—changes the nutritional picture significantly, but as so many of the recipes in this book prove, potatoes need not swim in fat to be rich in flavor.

PROFILING THE POTATO: TYPES

To most cooks, until very recently, a potato was a potato was a potato—and probably an Idaho to boot. While there is no reason to malign the sturdy Idaho, it would be a shame to ignore the cornucopia of potatoes now becoming available to the consumer. Some are beginning to appear on the shelves of local supermarkets and greengrocers; more esoteric varieties can be found in specialty and gourmet shops, or ordered by mail; and to the intrepid gardener, literally thousands of varieties are available for cultivation.

In this book, potatoes are characterized as waxy, floury, or all-purpose. Low in starch and high in water content, waxy potatoes are normally used for boiling, steaming, pan-frying, and in salads. Floury potatoes, on the other hand, are starchier and lower in water, and are at their finest when baked, mashed, or deep fried. In all-purpose potatoes, the starch and water content are roughly in balance. To determine the character of a mystery potato, use this simple test: Combine eleven parts water with one part salt and add the potato. If it sinks, it is floury; if it floats, it is waxy.

In addition, most American potatoes fall into one of four basic categories: russets, long whites, round whites, and round reds. Beyond the basic categories, there are the sweet potatoes, novelties, and new potatoes. Each will be explained in turn.

Russets: Called Idahos no matter where they're grown, oblong, brown-skinned russets are the familiar accompaniment to steaks and salads across America. Their floury texture stands up well to baking, while their irregular shape and prominent eyes make them better suited to dishes that don't require regularity of form—mashed potatoes, for example. Varieties include Russet Burbank, Norgold Russet, Centennial Russet, and Butte.

Long Whites: Characterized by a thin skin, smooth texture, elliptical shape, and nearly invisible eyes, these slightly yellow potatoes are considered all-purpose and are especially good when steamed or boiled. White Rose is a popular variety.

Round Whites: Deriving their name from an ivory color and round shape, these waxy, low-starch potatoes are perfect for boiling. Their thin skins have a surprisingly creamy texture when cooked. Kennebec, Katahdin, Superior, Norchip, Irish Cobbler, Monoma, Sebago, Ontario, and Chippewa are some well-known varieties.

Round Reds: Some are indeed round, while others are slightly oblong; many are red, though some are closer to ecru. Whatever their shape and hue, all varieties of these waxy, smooth-skinned potatoes are top-notch choices for boiling. Varietal names often reflect the potatoes' color, as in Red Pontiac, Red La Soda, La Rouge, Red Bliss, and Red McClure. (Look for Norland and Viking as well.)

Sweet Potatoes: They look like potatoes, cook like potatoes, and indeed, via the Arawak Indian word *batata*, gave their name to potatoes, but in truth they are not technically potatoes. Nevertheless, just like the potato, sweet potatoes have won a place in our hearts. Members of the morning glory family, flavor-rich sweet potatoes deserve to make more than a once-yearly Thanksgiving appearance. Varieties include Jersey Gold, Red Garnet, and Nugget. While most people use the words *sweet potato* and *yam* interchangeably, in fact yams, like regular potatoes, belong to the nightshade family. Though they can be substituted for sweet potatoes in most recipes, yams are sweeter and slightly starchier. Popular types are Gold Rush, Centennial, and Porto Rico.

INTRODUCTION

Novelty Potatoes: As a group, the newly introduced varieties are starchy and highly adaptable, the perfect foils for onion and garlic, chilies of all kinds, and a host of exotic spices. One of the more intriguing newcomers is Lady Finger, a long, thin arc of a tuber, with waxy flesh and a pale yellow skin. Marvelous in salads, Lady Finger can withstand even the most acidic vinaigrette. Not for the faint of heart, Peruvian Purple is tiny—barely an inch long—with a prune-purple skin, startling purple-blue flesh, and a musty, earthy flavor that reminds some of its boosters of truffles. The skin of the lovely Pink-Pearl is a delicate orange-pink, complemented by a firm, floury flesh ideal for baking.

New Potatoes: Any newly harvested tuber falls under the rubric of new potato, though unscrupulous grocers may try to pass off some varieties of round red as "new." Don't be fooled: Real new potatoes are available only from late winter through midsummer, and their thin skin will flake readily when rubbed.

POTATO COOKERY

One of the potato's greatest assets is its culinary adaptability. Here are suggestions for obtaining the best results from each cooking method.

Baking: Potato proponents are an opinionated lot—put two or more in a room together and inevitably a friendly argument will develop over the best methods of preparation. Baking, in theory the simplest method of all, elicits the most heated debate. Some extol the microwave for its ease; others condemn it as too drying; the same goes for cooking in aluminum foil, which is really steaming and can result in an unpleasantly soggy skin.

Many people believe that a basic approach yields the most satisfactory results: Pierce the skin in a few places with the tines of a fork to allow steam to escape, then bake the potato on a rack in a preheated 400°F. oven for 45 to 60 minutes, depending on its size. When the flesh responds to a squeeze (protect your hand with a kitchen towel or oven mitt!), the potato is fully baked.

Boiling: To peel or not to peel before cooking—that is the preeminent question when boiling potatoes. Though peeling cooked potatoes takes a little more time (you'll want to wait for them to cool a bit, and it helps to dry them in a hot oven), the technique pays off in nutrients and flavor preserved. With skin or without, place the potatoes in a saucepan with just enough water to cover and bring to a boil over high heat. (If

you like, you can add 1 teaspoon of salt per quart of water.) Reduce the heat to low; cover and simmer whole large potatoes for 30 to 40 minutes and cut potatoes for 15 to 25. Boiled potatoes are done when a fork passes easily through the flesh. (For extra flavor, try substituting homemade stock for the water.) Drain in a colander and, if you plan to peel them, cool until just comfortable to handle.

Steaming: Steaming works best on waxy boiling-style potatoes. Its major advantage over boiling is its preservation of additional nutrients. Place unpeeled potatoes in a steamer basket or rack in a pot over two inches of boiling water. (The water shouldn't touch the potatoes.) Cover and steam for 15 to 30 minutes, depending on the size of the potatoes. The flavor of steamed potatoes can be subtly enhanced with the addition of seasonings to the water. Try garlic, lemon peel, juniper berries, peppercorns, fresh nutmeg, or whatever else you find appealing. Or substitute wine, homemade stock, or vegetable or fruit juices for water.

Pan-Roasting: Pan-roasting is one of the easiest and most appealing ways to cook potatoes, especially if they accompany roasted meat. Properly roasted potatoes should have a crisp, brown exterior and a buttery interior. On their own, place the potatoes sliced or chunked in a shallow pan; brush them with butter, margarine, oil, or—for sinfully rich results—chicken fat, and bake at 400°F. for 45 minutes, or until fork-tender, stirring occasionally. When cooking with a roast, add the potatoes 1 hour before the meat is done, turning to coat them with the pan drippings. In either case, feel free to add seasonings—salt and freshly ground pepper, of course, but also aromatic herbs such as rosemary and sage, or garlic, either whole in the clove or minced.

All potatoes should be scrubbed and patted dry before cooking, with one exception: The tender skin of new potatoes will disintegrate under the scrub brush, so wipe it gently with a damp paper towel instead.

And a final warning: Green-hued potatoes derive their color not from immaturity but from sun exposure, which causes them to develop surface concentrations of the toxin solanine. Don't buy them; if you *have* bought them, throw them out.

STORAGE

Even after they leave the market, potatoes retain their connection to the earth, most arriving home with soil still dusting their skins. Indeed, potatoes do keep somewhat longer in this slightly "dirty" state, as any

INTRODUCTION

gardener will tell you. When storing potatoes there are three essential words to bear in mind: *dry*, *dark*, and *cool*. Never wash potatoes before storage: This will only hasten decomposition. And make sure your potatoes rest in the dark: Exposure to strong light—whether from the sun or an overhead fixture—can trigger the formation of solanine, rendering the potatoes inedible. Most important, keep them cool—38 to 40° F. for regular potatoes, and 50 to 60°F. for sweets. Overly warm temperatures will give you dry, wrinkled potatoes with all the appeal of an old sock ball. Don't, however, store potatoes in an uninsulated mud room or pantry, or in the refrigerator or freezer: At freezing or near-freezing temperatures, the potatoes' starches are converted to sugars, producing tubers that are mushy, overly sweet, and often discolored. (To prolong the life of sweet potatoes, cure them first for one to two weeks in a warm, humid place—85 to 90°F. and 80 to 90 percent humidity.) Mature potatoes will keep for several months under the right conditions—yet another endearing attribute of the world's most popular vegetable.

The once-wild root ball that had its origins in the pre-Colombian Andes is now one of the world's most adaptable foods: Wrapped with tender prosciutto, or gently tossed in a rosemary vinaigrette with the spring's first fiddleheads, the potato is transformed into something ethereal and elegant; bubbling in a rich potato and corn chowder or serving as the unexpected base for a fiery chili, it is heartiness incarnate. It lends its unique texture to some of the world's most enticing breads and rolls, and in recipes like purple potato chips and fried potato curls it is a nearly irresistible snack food. The intent of this book is to expand your potato repertoire, and to celebrate what is truly a golden age for the glorious tuber.

HORS D'OEUVRES AND APPETIZERS

Mashed Potato and Garlic Dip

Layered Sweet Potato-Vegetable Terrine

Prosciutto-Wrapped Potato Fingers

Sausage-Stuffed Potatoes

Savory Potato-Stuffed Mushrooms

Potato-Leek Tartlets

Potato Skins

Potato-Shrimp Canapés

Caraway-Potato Sticks

Potato Pissaladière

Cheesy Potato Puffs

Potato and Cod Cakes

Roasted Purple Potatoes with Caviar and Sour Cream

Grilled Purple Potato and Vegetable Skewers

Potato, Smoked Salmon, and Spinach Timbales

Marinated Potatoes and Sun-Dried Tomatoes

CHAPTER ONE

MASHED POTATO AND GARLIC DIP

Yukon potatoes have a buttery flavor and are available in many markets. Here they are combined with garbanzo beans and garlic in a robust dip. This dip also makes a sophisticated sandwich spread.

Makes 3 cups dip.

1½ pounds Yukon gold potatoes, drained and rinsed
One 10½-ounce can garbanzo beans, drained and rinsed
¼ cup olive oil
4 garlic cloves, crushed
1 teaspoon salt
¼ cup chopped parsley
Toasted pita triangles

Place the potatoes and enough water to cover in a 2-quart saucepan over high heat and bring to a boil. Reduce the heat to low; cover and simmer 15 to 20 minutes, or until the potatoes are tender.

Meanwhile, in a food processor or blender, blend the garbanzo beans, olive oil, garlic cloves, and salt.

Drain the potatoes, reserving ½ cup of potato water. In a large bowl, mash the potatoes; add the garbanzo mixture, the reserved ½ cup potato water, and the chopped parsley, and combine until well mixed.

Serve the dip with the toasted pita triangles.

LAYERED SWEET POTATO-
VEGETABLE TERRINE

Here is a vegetable pâté made up of colorful layers of sweet potato and spinach with zucchini, which is a great dish for buffet serving. Cut the terrine into slices, slightly overlapping them, and arrange on a platter. If you like, serve with a purée of roasted red peppers.

Serves 12.

4 large sweet potatoes
3 tablespoons olive oil
3 pounds zucchini, chopped
1 large onion, diced
2 large garlic cloves, minced
4 cups chopped fresh spinach
4 large eggs
3 cups dried bread crumbs
2 teaspoons salt
¼ teaspoon freshly ground black pepper
¼ teaspoon ground nutmeg
2 tablespoons chopped parsley
2 tablespoons butter or margarine
1 tablespoon brown sugar
¼ teaspoon ground cinnamon

Place the sweet potatoes and enough water to cover in a 3-quart saucepan over high heat and bring to a boil. Reduce the heat to low; cover and simmer 30 minutes, or until the sweet potatoes are tender. Drain.

Meanwhile, in a 4-quart saucepan over medium heat, heat the oil; cook the zucchini, onion, and garlic for 5 minutes. Add the spinach; cook 5 minutes longer, or until the vegetables are tender, stirring them occasionally.

In a food processor or blender, blend the vegetable mixture until smooth. In a large bowl, beat the eggs; stir in the bread crumbs, 1½ teaspoons of the salt, pepper, nutmeg, and puréed vegetable mixture.

CHAPTER ONE

When the sweet potatoes are cool enough to handle, peel. In a medium bowl, mash the potatoes; stir in the parsley, butter, brown sugar, cinnamon, and the remaining ½ teaspoon salt.

Preheat the oven to 325° F. Grease a 9-×5-inch loaf pan. Spread one-half of vegetable mixture in the pan. Cover with the sweet potato mixture spread in an even layer, and top with the remaining vegetable mixture. Cover the pan with foil. Place the loaf pan in a shallow baking pan; fill the baking pan with hot water to come halfway up the sides of the loaf pan. Bake 1 hour and 15 minutes, or until the loaf feels firm and when tested a knife inserted in the center comes out clean.

Completely cool the loaf in the pan. Refrigerate until ready to serve. To serve, invert the loaf onto a serving platter; cut into slices.

Prosciutto-Wrapped Potato Fingers

As simple as these hors d'oeuvres may seem, they impart considerable flavor, due in large measure to the salty smokiness of the prosciutto. Guests will love them so much, you may want to double the recipe.

Makes 16.

2 large baking potatoes
¼ pound thinly sliced prosciutto
1 tablespoon olive oil

Preheat the oven to 450° F. Cut each potato in half lengthwise, and then into 4 spears each to make a total of 8 wedges. Cut the prosciutto into 4-×1-inch pieces. Wrap a piece of prosciutto around each potato wedge, and place on a jelly-roll pan. Brush with the olive oil. Bake 15 minutes, turning once, until the potatoes are tender.

Sausage-Stuffed Potatoes

Delicious and easy to make, sausage-stuffed potatoes also lend themselves to advance preparation. To reheat, wrap in foil and bake in a 325° F. oven for 25 minutes, or until heated through.

Serves 4.

4 large Idaho potatoes
One 12-ounce package bulk pork sausage
¼ cup chopped parsley
¼ cup shredded Cheddar cheese (optional)

Preheat the oven to 400° F. Scrub the potatoes well. Bake for 45 minutes, or until they are tender.

Meanwhile, in a 10-inch skillet over medium heat, cook the sausage until well browned, breaking it up into small pieces with a fork. Remove to paper towels to drain.

Cut a thin lengthwise slice off the top of each potato. Scrape the pulp into a large bowl and discard the top skin. Scoop out the rest of the potato pulp, leaving a ¼-inch-thick shell. Toss with the sausage and parsley, breaking up clumps with a fork.

Reduce the oven temperature to 350° F. Spoon the mixture into the potato shells, mounding it generously. Place the stuffed potatoes on a small cookie sheet. Sprinkle each with 1 tablespoon of the cheese. Bake 15 minutes, or until heated through.

SAVORY POTATO-STUFFED MUSHROOMS

Many stuffed mushroom hors d'oeuvres recipes rely on sausage or other mushrooms as the filling. The combination of potatoes and cream cheese in this recipe makes an unusual, luscious stuffing, while the hot pepper sauce adds spiciness.

Makes 1 dozen stuffed mushrooms.

½ pound Yukon gold potatoes, peeled and cut up
12 large mushrooms, each about 2 inches in diameter
3 tablespoons butter or margarine
4 ounces cream cheese*
3 tablespoons chopped chives
¾ teaspoon salt
¼ teaspoon hot red pepper sauce
1 tablespoon olive oil

In a 2-quart saucepan over high heat, bring the potatoes with enough water to cover to a boil. Reduce the heat to low; cover and simmer 15 minutes, or until the potatoes are tender. Drain. Mash the potatoes.

Meanwhile, remove the stems from the mushrooms; chop the stems and set aside. Carefully scoop out the center of each mushroom cap with a spoon, leaving a ½-inch shell.

In a 10-inch skillet over medium heat, heat the butter until hot, and in it cook the chopped mushroom stems 3 minutes, or until tender. Remove from heat; stir in the mashed potatoes, cream cheese, 2 tablespoons of the chives, salt, and hot pepper sauce.

Preheat the oven to 450° F. Fill each mushroom cap with some of the potato mixture, mounding it slightly. Brush the stuffed mushrooms with some of the oil. Bake 10 minutes, or until lightly golden. Garnish each mushroom cap with remaining chives.

*Or, use *4 ounces chive cream cheese* and omit the chopped chives.

Potato-Leek Tartlets

You can use the green part of the leek—the leaves—as well as the white bulb end in the filling for these tarts. They make a wonderful first course, as appealing to the eye as to the palate.

Makes 6 tartlets.

CRUST

1 cup whole-wheat flour
1 cup all-purpose flour
¾ teaspoon dried thyme leaves
½ teaspoon salt
¾ cup butter or margarine, melted

FILLING

3 tablespoons butter or margarine
½ pound all-purpose potatoes, peeled and diced (about 2 cups)
1 large leek, chopped (about 2 cups)
1 small red bell pepper, diced
1 large garlic clove, crushed
1 cup half-and-half
1 large egg
1 teaspoon salt
½ teaspoon dried thyme leaves
¼ teaspoon freshly ground black pepper

Preheat the oven to 375° F. In a large bowl, combine the whole-wheat flour, all-purpose flour, thyme, and salt. Stir in the melted butter until well blended. Press the mixture into six 4½-inch fluted tart pans. Place on a cookie sheet. Bake 15 minutes. Remove from the oven.

Meanwhile, prepare the filling: In a 12-inch skillet over medium heat, melt the butter or margarine, and in it cook the diced potatoes about 5 minutes. Add the leek, red pepper, and garlic; cook 5 minutes, or until the vegetables are tender, stirring occasionally.

CHAPTER ONE

In a large bowl, combine the half-and-half, egg, salt, thyme, and black pepper. Divide the vegetable filling among the tarts; pour the egg mixture over the vegetables. Bake the tartlets 20 minutes, or until the filling is slightly puffed and the crust is golden.

POTATO SKINS

A popular dish these days, these crispy potato skins can be served as a snack or with a meal. Placed in a basket on the buffet table, they set a casual tone for a Sunday afternoon gathering or a barbecue.

Serves 6.

3 large baking potatoes
Salt
Freshly ground black pepper

Preheat the oven to 425° F. Scrub the potatoes well; prick with a fork. Bake the potatoes 1 hour, or until tender.

Cut each potato crosswise in half. Scoop out the pulp, leaving a ¼-inch-thick shell. Cut each potato half lengthwise into 4 pieces. Place the pieces on a cookie sheet. Sprinkle lightly with salt and pepper. Bake 30 minutes, or until crisp, turning once.

Serve the potato skins with sour cream, guacamole, chili, or other favorite dips.

POTATO-SHRIMP CANAPÉS

Grated potatoes are the coating for the shrimp-herb mixture in this starter dish. The patties are then fried and served with a mustardy sauce. You will find that the assorted flavors balance each other beautifully. The sauce can also be made in advance.

Serves 8.

CANAPÉS

2 pounds baking potatoes, peeled
½ pound small shrimp, peeled and deveined
1 tablespoon snipped chives
2 teaspoons lemon juice
½ teaspoon salt
¼ teaspoon freshly ground black pepper
4 cups peanut oil for frying

RÉMOULADE SAUCE

⅓ cup country-style or coarse-grain mustard
¼ cup finely chopped parsley
¼ cup finely chopped celery
2 tablespoons minced dill pickle
1 tablespoon red wine vinegar
1 small garlic clove, minced

In a food processor with the grater blade attached, or with a mandoline, grate the potatoes. Press out any liquid from the potatoes and place them on paper towels to drain.

In a medium bowl, toss the shrimp, chives, lemon juice, salt, and pepper. In the palm of your hand, place ¼ cup grated potatoes. Top with some of the shrimp mixture and another ¼ cup grated potatoes; set aside. Repeat with remaining potatoes and shrimp mixture. Sprinkle lightly with salt and pepper. Form into patties.

In a 10-inch skillet over medium-high heat, heat the peanut oil to 375° F. Carefully add the potato patties. Fry the patties until golden, about 3 minutes total. Remove to paper towels to drain.

Meanwhile, prepare the sauce: In a small bowl, stir together the mustard, parsley, celery, pickle, vinegar, and garlic until well blended. Serve each canapé with a dollop of *rémoulade* sauce.

CARAWAY-POTATO STICKS

Spears of potatoes are sprinkled here with caraway seeds, then roasted until crisp and golden. You will find yourself eating these sticks like potato chips.

Makes 30 sticks, serving 6–8 as an hors d'oeuvre.

2 pounds baking potatoes
1 tablespoon olive oil
½ teaspoon caraway seeds
1 teaspoon salt
1 teaspoon paprika
½ cup sour cream

Preheat the oven to 425° F. Slice each unpeeled potato lengthwise into 10 wedges (about ½ inch thick). Place in a roasting pan. Combine the oil and caraway seeds; brush the potatoes with mixture. Sprinkle with the salt and paprika.

Bake about 40 minutes, or until golden and crisp, turning once. Serve with the sour cream for dipping.

Potato Pissaladière

In France this open-faced tart is commonly baked in a round and frequently topped with anchovies. I have added all-purpose potatoes (new potatoes are especially nice), and removed the anchovies. The pie has a country feel to it, and can be cut into larger servings and served with a salad as an alternative to quiche.

Makes 18 hors d'oeuvres.

½ cup milk
¼ cup butter or margarine
1 package active dry yeast
1¾ cups whole-wheat flour
1 cup all-purpose flour
2 teaspoons salt
2 large eggs
¼ cup olive oil
¾ pound all-purpose potatoes, peeled and sliced
1 large tomato, sliced
1 small onion, thinly sliced
¼ cup pitted black olives, chopped

In a 2-quart saucepan over low heat, heat the milk and butter until warm (120° to 130° F.). In a large bowl, combine the yeast, flours, and 1 teaspoon of the salt. Stir the warm milk mixture into the flour mixture with the eggs until well blended. Cover; let rise in a warm place about 1 hour, until doubled in bulk.

Meanwhile, in a 10-inch skillet over medium heat, heat 2 tablespoons of the oil, and cook the potato slices until tender and lightly browned.

Preheat the oven to 400° F. Grease a 13- × 9-inch baking pan. With floured fingers, press dough into bottom of pan. Brush 1 tablespoon of the olive oil over the dough. Arrange the potatoes, tomato and onion slices, and olives on the dough; brush with the remaining 1 tablespoon olive oil and sprinkle with remaining 1 tablespoon salt. Bake 15 to 20 minutes, or until the crust is golden and crisp. Cut into 3- × 1½-inch pieces.

CHEESY POTATO PUFFS

Crisp on the outside, moist and delicious on the inside, these cheesy potato puffs are best served with a full-flavored mustard.

Makes 14 hors d'oeuvres.

1 cup mashed potatoes
½ cup grated Cheddar cheese
¼ cup finely chopped parsley
1 teaspoon caraway seeds
¾ teaspoon salt
¼ teaspoon cayenne pepper
½ cup dried bread crumbs
1 large egg, beaten
3 cups vegetable oil for frying
Spicy hot mustard

In a medium bowl, combine the mashed potatoes, Cheddar cheese, parsley, caraway seeds, salt, and cayenne pepper. Shape the mixture, 1 tablespoonful at a time, into balls. Roll the potato balls in the bread crumbs, then in the beaten egg, and again in the bread crumbs.

In a 2-quart saucepan over medium heat, heat the vegetable oil to 325°F. on a deep-fat thermometer (or heat oil in deep-fryer or electric skillet at 325°F.). Fry the potato balls 2 to 3 minutes, until lightly browned and crisp. Remove the potato puffs to paper towels to drain. Serve immediately with spicy hot mustard.

POTATO AND COD CAKES

Fresh cod fillets are an expensive ingredient, so frugal cooks may like the way this flavorful recipe stretches them out. These tasty appetizers can be shaped into four round patties and served as a main course as well.

Makes 8 appetizers.

3 Yukon gold potatoes, peeled and cut into large chunks
8 ounces fresh cod fillets
1 large egg
¼ cup chopped fresh dill
¼ cup dried bread crumbs
3 tablespoons prepared horseradish
2 tablespoons grated onion
1½ teaspoons salt
¼ teaspoon freshly ground black pepper
1 tablespoon butter or margarine
1 tablespoon vegetable oil

CREAMY DILL SAUCE
½ cup sour cream
1 tablespoon chopped fresh dill
1 tablespoon prepared horseradish
2 tablespoons lemon juice

Dill sprigs for garnish

Place the potatoes and enough water to cover in a 3-quart saucepan over high heat and bring to a boil. Reduce the heat to low; cover and simmer 10 minutes. Add the cod; cook 5 minutes longer, or until the fish and potatoes are tender. Drain. Remove any bones from the fish.

In a large bowl, mash the potatoes and the cod. Stir in the egg, dill, bread crumbs, horseradish, onion, salt, and pepper. Shape the mixture into 8 round patties, about 2 inches in diameter. The patties may be chilled until ready to cook.

In a 12-inch skillet over medium heat, heat the butter and oil until hot. Add the patties and cook about 5 minutes, or until golden on both sides, turning once.

Meanwhile, prepare the sauce: In a small bowl, combine the sour cream, dill, horseradish, and lemon juice until well blended.

Serve the potato and cod cakes with a dollop of Creamy Dill Sauce on each. Garnish with the dill sprigs.

ROASTED PURPLE POTATOES WITH CAVIAR AND SOUR CREAM

Using purple potatoes instead of red potatoes in this recipe makes for a delicious variation on a classic combination. To reduce fat and cholesterol, consider substituting light, low-calorie sour cream. Serve elegantly, with plates and forks.

Makes 24 hors d'oeuvres.

1 pound purple potatoes
2 tablespoons olive oil
¼ cup sour cream or plain yogurt
2 tablespoons red lumpfish caviar
Small dill sprigs for garnish

Preheat the oven to 425° F.

Cut the potatoes crosswise in half and toss with the olive oil. Place the potatoes, cut side up, in an 11-× 8-inch baking pan. Roast the potatoes 15 to 20 minutes, or until just tender when pierced with a fork. Cool the potatoes about 30 minutes.

To serve, top each potato half with ½ teaspoon sour cream; sprinkle with ¼ teaspoon caviar. Garnish with a dill sprig.

GRILLED PURPLE POTATO
AND VEGETABLE SKEWERS

These skewers offer a lively contrast of colors and have a slightly Provençal taste. Consider grilling them over hot coals as a main barbecue course in warm weather. Yellow summer squash can be substituted for the red peppers.

Makes 10 appetizer skewers.

1½ pounds purple potatoes, peeled and cut into ¾-inch
   chunks
2 cups pearl onions, peeled
1 large red bell pepper, cored, seeded, and cut into ¾-inch
   chunks
¼ cup olive oil
2 tablespoons chopped fresh thyme leaves or 2 teaspoons
   dried thyme
2 tablespoons balsamic vinegar
1 teaspoon salt

Preheat the broiler. On ten 6-inch-long wooden skewers, alternately thread the potato chunks, pearl onions, and red pepper. Place in medium-sized baking dish or deep platter.

In a small bowl, combine the olive oil, thyme, vinegar, and salt. Pour the mixture over the skewers in the dish. Let marinate for 20 minutes, turning occasionally.

Place the skewers on the rack of a broiler pan and reserve the marinade. Broil 3 to 5 inches from the heat source, for 8 to 10 minutes, turning occasionally and brushing with the marinade.

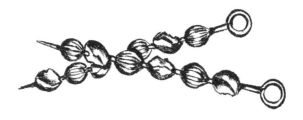

CHAPTER ONE

POTATO, SMOKED SALMON, AND SPINACH TIMBALES

Consider serving these rather sophisticated timbales, or molds, as a first course to an elegant dinner of roast beef. The timbales can be prepared several hours in advance and should be reheated in the waterbath in which they bake.

Serves 4.

1 cup mashed potatoes
½ cup minced smoked salmon
½ cup frozen chopped spinach, thawed and squeezed dry
½ cup half-and-half
3 large eggs
1 tablespoon chopped fresh dill
¼ teaspoon salt
⅛ teaspoon freshly ground black pepper
Spinach leaves and lemon twists for garnish

In a large bowl, combine the mashed potatoes, smoked salmon, spinach, half-and-half, eggs, dill, salt, and pepper until well blended.

Preheat the oven to 350° F. Grease four 6-ounce custard cups or eight 3-ounce timbale molds. Divide the mixture among the prepared cups, then place cups in a baking pan. Fill the pan with boiling water to come halfway up the sides of the cups.

Bake 45 minutes, or until a knife inserted in the center comes out clean. Invert the cups onto serving plates. Garnish with the spinach leaves and lemon twists.

MARINATED POTATOES AND SUN-DRIED TOMATOES

This easy appetizer lends itself to being made in advance; the longer the potatoes marinate, the better.

Serves 4.

1½ pounds red potatoes, cut into 1-inch chunks
½ cup sun-dried tomatoes, finely chopped
¼ cup chopped fresh basil or 2 teaspoons dried basil
¼ cup olive oil
¼ cup red wine vinegar
1 large garlic clove, thinly sliced
¼ teaspoon salt
¼ teaspoon crushed red pepper
½ cup pitted black olives, sliced
Endive leaves

Place the potatoes and enough water to cover in a 2-quart sauce-pan over high heat and bring to a boil. Reduce the heat to low. Cover and simmer 20 minutes, or until the potatoes are tender. Drain.

In a large bowl, combine the sun-dried tomatoes, basil, olive oil, vinegar, garlic, salt, and crushed red pepper. Add the drained potatoes and the olives; toss to mix well. Serve the potato mixture over the endive leaves.

CHAPTER TWO

SOUPS

Potato-Corn Chowder

Potato and Salmon Soup with Chives

Potato Peel and Garlic Soup

Potato Cucumber Soup with Dill

Sweet Potato and Turnip Soup

Cold Sweet Potato and Cranberry Soup

Potato and Wild Mushroom Bisque

Chilled Potato Gazpacho

Cream of Sweet Potato and Thyme Soup

Kohlrabi and Potato Soup with Garlic Croutons

Potato Leek Soup

Caribbean-Style Potato Clam Chowder

Potato and Cheddar Soup

Red Bliss Potato and Oyster Chowder

Black Bean and Potato Soup

Purée of Potato and Carrot Soup

Potato Beet Borscht

Cold Potato and Cantaloupe Soup

POTATO-CORN CHOWDER

A lovely, rich soup with a unique flavor, this chowder can be served as an enticing first course. Add pieces of cooked shrimp or lobster to make it even more special.

Serves 6.

⅓ cup butter or margarine
1 pound all-purpose potatoes, peeled and diced
2 celery stalks, diced
1 small green bell pepper, seeded and diced
1 small onion, diced
3 tablespoons all-purpose flour
2 tablespoons sweet paprika
2 cups water
One 16-ounce can corn, drained
2 vegetable bouillon cubes
2 cups half-and-half

In a 4-quart saucepan over medium heat, melt the butter, and in it cook the potatoes, celery, green pepper, and onion 10 minutes, stirring occasionally. Stir in the flour and paprika; cook 1 minute, stirring constantly. Add the water, corn, and bouillon cubes. Bring to a boil over high heat; reduce the heat to low; cover and simmer 15 minutes, or until the vegetables are tender.

Stir in the half-and-half. Over low heat, heat through, but do not let boil.

Potato and Salmon Soup with Chives

To dress up this creamy soup for company, coat thinly sliced lemon with finely chopped dill and float a slice or two on each serving. Serve it warm in winter and cold in summer—it's always delicious!

Serves 4.

2 tablespoons butter or margarine
1 pound all-purpose potatoes, peeled and cut into chunks
8 ounces salmon, boned, skinned, and cut into 1-inch chunks
8 ounces shallots, chopped
1½ cups water
1 cup fish stock or broth
1 teaspoon salt
¼ teaspoon freshly ground black pepper
1 cup half-and-half or milk
2 tablespoons snipped fresh chives
2 teaspoons lemon juice

In a 3-quart saucepan over medium heat, melt the butter, and in it cook the potatoes until lightly browned, about 5 minutes, stirring occasionally.

Stir in the salmon and shallots; cook 5 minutes longer, stirring occasionally. Add the water, fish stock, salt, and pepper. Bring to a boil over high heat. Reduce the heat to low; cover and simmer 15 minutes, stirring occasionally.

In a blender or food processor, blend the mixture in batches until smooth. Return to the saucepan. Stir in the half-and-half, chives, and lemon juice. Over low heat, heat through, but do not let boil. Serve warm, or chill to serve cold.

POTATO PEEL AND GARLIC SOUP

Here is a nutty and robust soup that boasts the multiple virtues of being quick, easy, and economical to make. It is particularly attractive when served in lively Mediterranean-style crockery. Sourdough bread makes for a nice accompaniment.

Serves 2.

2 tablespoons vegetable oil
2 cups chopped potato skins (from 3 large leftover
    baked potatoes)
2 large garlic cloves, crushed
One 13¾-ounce can chicken broth
1 teaspoon salt
¼ teaspoon freshly ground black pepper
¼ cup chopped parsley

In a 2-quart saucepan over medium-high heat, heat the oil, and in it cook the potato skins until browned on both sides, stirring frequently. Add the garlic; cook over medium heat for 1 minute.

Stir in the chicken broth, salt, and pepper. Bring to a boil over high heat. Reduce the heat to low; cover and simmer 10 minutes, stirring occasionally.

In a blender or food processor, blend the mixture in batches until smooth. Stir in the parsley and serve.

POTATO CUCUMBER SOUP WITH DILL

Adding potatoes to a classic cucumber and dill combination gives this soup an Old World heartiness that's very appealing.

Serves 4.

2 tablespoons butter or margarine
3 medium all-purpose potatoes, peeled and chopped
1 large cucumber (about 8 ounces) peeled, seeded, and diced
1 small garlic clove, crushed
One 13¾-ounce can chicken broth
1 cup water
2 tablespoons chopped fresh dill
1 teaspoon salt
1 tablespoon lemon juice
Plain yogurt (optional)
Dill sprigs for garnish

In a 3-quart saucepan over medium heat, heat the butter, and in it cook the potatoes about 10 minutes, stirring occasionally. Add the cucumber and garlic; cook 1 minute longer.

Stir in the chicken broth, water, dill, and salt. Bring to a boil over high heat. Reduce the heat to low; cover and simmer 10 minutes, stirring occasionally.

In a blender or food processor, coarsely purée the soup in batches. Return the soup to the saucepan. Stir in the lemon juice and heat through. If you like, top each serving with a dollop of yogurt. Garnish with dill sprigs.

CHAPTER TWO

Sweet Potato and Turnip Soup

Potatoes and turnips make a winning duet in this savory, nourishing peasant soup that's perfect for the fall.

Serves 6.

2 tablespoons butter or margarine
2 tablespoons vegetable oil
4 cups diced, peeled sweet potatoes (about 4 small potatoes)
3 cups diced, peeled white turnips (about 3 large turnips)
3 medium celery stalks, diced
2 large leeks, thinly sliced
4 cups water
2 vegetable bouillon cubes
1 teaspoon salt
¼ teaspoon cayenne pepper
¼ cup chopped parsley

In a 4-quart saucepan over medium heat, heat the butter and oil, and in it cook the sweet potatoes, turnips, celery, and leeks until the vegetables are lightly browned, about 10 minutes, stirring occasionally.

Add the water, bouillon cubes, salt, cayenne pepper, and parsley. Bring to a boil over high heat. Reduce the heat to low; cover and simmer 25 to 30 minutes, or until the vegetables are tender, stirring the mixture occasionally.

COLD SWEET POTATO AND CRANBERRY SOUP

Combining sweet potatoes with tart cranberries, orange, and ginger makes a soup that is autumnal and festive at the same time. To make a complete meal—especially during the holiday season—serve with turkey sandwiches.

Serves 4.

2 pounds sweet potatoes, peeled and cut into large chunks
2½ cups orange juice
One 16-ounce can whole berry cranberry sauce
2 tablespoons minced crystallized ginger
1 tablespoon grated orange peel
¼ teaspoon ground cinnamon

Place the sweet potatoes and enough water to cover in a 2-quart saucepan over high heat and bring to a boil. Reduce the heat to low; cover and simmer 15 to 20 minutes, or until the sweet potatoes are tender. Drain.

In a blender or food processor, purée the cooked sweet potatoes with the orange juice, cranberry sauce, and ginger until smooth. Stir in the grated orange peel and cinnamon. Transfer the soup to a bowl and refrigerate until ready to serve.

POTATO AND
WILD MUSHROOM BISQUE

This wonderful soup has plenty of texture and flavor contrast, and it's great served with crusty French bread. Cremini mushrooms, perhaps more difficult to find than *shiitake*, are well worth the search. Look for them at specialty gourmet food markets.

Serves 4.

4 tablespoons salted butter or margarine
½ pound cremini or shiitake *mushrooms, chopped (¾ cup)*
¾ cup diced onion
1¼ pounds all-purpose potatoes, peeled and cut in large
  chunks
One 13¾-ounce can chicken broth
1 teaspoon salt
¼ teaspoon freshly ground black pepper
1 cup milk

In a 4-quart saucepan over medium heat, melt the butter, and in it cook the mushrooms and onion about 5 minutes, stirring occasionally. Add the potato chunks, chicken broth, salt, and pepper. Bring to a boil over high heat. Reduce the heat to low; cover and simmer 20 minutes, until the potatoes are tender, stirring occasionally.

In a food processor or blender, purée 1 cup of the soup. Return to the saucepan. Add the milk, and heat through.

CHILLED POTATO GAZPACHO

This low-calorie, healthy soup is refreshing on a hot summer day. Garnish it with additional finely chopped peppers (red or green), red onion, or diced cucumber from the recipe.

Serves 6.

1 pound ripe tomatoes, peeled, seeded, and chopped
1 cup cooked potatoes, chopped (2 medium all-purpose
potatoes)
1 medium red or green bell pepper, seeded and chopped
1 small red onion, chopped
1 small cucumber, peeled, seeded, and chopped
1 small jalapeño pepper, seeded and chopped
2 large garlic cloves
3 cups tomato juice
2 tablespoons red wine vinegar
2 tablespoons lime juice
¾ teaspoon salt
¼ teaspoon freshly ground black pepper
¼ cup chopped fresh coriander

In a blender or food processor, blend the tomatoes, potatoes, red or green pepper, onion, cucumber, jalapeño pepper, garlic, tomato juice, vinegar, lime juice, salt, and pepper until smooth. Refrigerate about 3 hours, or until chilled.

To serve, stir in the chopped coriander.

CREAM OF SWEET POTATO AND THYME SOUP

This rich soup has a magnificent color, and it makes an exquisite first course for an autumn or winter dinner. To throw caution entirely to the winds, garnish not with yogurt, but with sour cream.

Serves 4.

2 tablespoons butter or margarine
3 medium sweet potatoes, peeled and cut into ½-inch cubes
    (3 cups)
3 scallions, sliced
One 13¾-ounce can chicken broth
1 cup water
2 teaspoons chopped fresh thyme leaves or ¾ teaspoon
    dried thyme
2 teaspoons salt
¼ teaspoon freshly ground black pepper
2 cups half-and-half
Plain yogurt for garnish (optional)
Thyme sprigs for garnish

In a 3-quart saucepan over medium heat, melt the butter, and in it cook the sweet potatoes and scallions until the potatoes are lightly browned, stirring occasionally.

Add the chicken broth, water, thyme, salt, and pepper. Bring to a boil over high heat. Reduce the heat to low; cover and simmer 15 minutes, stirring occasionally.

In a blender or food processor, purée the soup in batches. Return it to the saucepan. Add the half-and-half; heat through. If you like, serve with a dollop of yogurt and garnish with thyme sprigs.

KOHLRABI AND POTATO SOUP WITH GARLIC CROUTONS

Kohlrabi, a root vegetable popular in Central Europe, is usually available in the spring and summer. The flavor is a cross between cabbage and a mild turnip.

Serves 6.

3 tablespoons vegetable oil
1 pound all-purpose potatoes, peeled and diced
2 celery stalks, diced
2 pounds kohlrabi, peeled and diced
2 large garlic cloves, minced
2 cups water
One 13¾-ounce can chicken broth
1 tablespoon snipped chives
2 teaspoons salt
¼ teaspoon freshly ground black pepper

GARLIC CROUTONS

3 tablespoons butter or margarine
1 large garlic clove, minced
One 5-inch-long piece Italian bread, cut into ¾-inch cubes
*   (about 3 cups)*

In a 3-quart saucepan over high heat, heat the oil, and in it cook the potatoes, celery, and kohlrabi until lightly browned, about 10 minutes, stirring occasionally. Add the garlic, and cook 1 minute longer.

Add the water, chicken broth, chives, salt, and pepper. Bring to a boil over high heat. Reduce the heat to low; cover and simmer 30 minutes, or until the vegetables are very tender, stirring occasionally.

Meanwhile, prepare the croutons: In a 12-inch skillet over medium heat, melt the butter, and in it cook the garlic about 1 minute, or until lightly browned, stirring constantly. Remove the garlic and add the bread cubes; cook about 3 minutes, or until the bread is lightly browned and crisp, stirring frequently.

In a food processor or blender, blend the soup mixture, one-third at a time, until smooth. Serve in bowls and garnish each serving with some of the Garlic Croutons.

POTATO LEEK SOUP

Potatoes and leeks are natural partners. Traditionally, when served cold, this soup is known as vichyssoise. Serve it hot if you feel like being cozy.

Serves 6.

3 tablespoons butter or margarine
2 large leeks, sliced (about 2 cups)
1 large garlic clove, crushed
1 pound all-purpose potatoes, peeled and cut into
    ¾-inch chunks
Two 13¾-ounce cans chicken broth
¼ teaspoon salt
⅛ teaspoon freshly ground black pepper

In a 3-quart saucepan over medium heat, melt the butter, and in it cook the leeks and garlic 5 minutes, stirring occasionally, until tender.

Add the potatoes, chicken broth, salt, and pepper. Bring to a boil over high heat. Reduce the heat to low; cover and simmer 15 minutes, or until the potatoes are tender. Serve the soup chunky, or purée it in a blender or food processor until smooth.

CARIBBEAN-STYLE POTATO CLAM CHOWDER

Potatoes, clams, and saffron combine here in a spicy tomato-and-clam-juice soup base reminiscent of island cooking. Consider serving this chowder as a main course, with a hearty bread and crisp green salad, perhaps one studded with orange or grapefruit segments.

Serves 6.

2 tablespoons vegetable oil
1 pound all-purpose potatoes, peeled and cut into ½-inch
  chunks
2 medium celery stalks, diced
1 medium onion, diced
2 large garlic cloves, crushed
¼ teaspoon ground saffron
One 28-ounce can whole tomatoes
Two 10-ounce cans clam juice
One 10-ounce can whole baby clams
¼ cup chopped parsley
½ teaspoon salt
¼ teaspoon freshly ground black pepper

In a 4-quart saucepan over medium heat, heat the oil, and in it cook the potatoes, celery, and onion until tender, about 10 minutes, stirring occasionally. Add the garlic and saffron, and cook 1 minute.

Add the tomatoes with their liquid, clam juice, clams with their liquid, parsley, salt, and pepper. Bring to a boil over high heat. Reduce the heat to low; cover and simmer 25 minutes, stirring occasionally.

POTATO AND CHEDDAR SOUP

To reheat this soup, warm it over low heat, stirring frequently to prevent curdling. Its gorgeous pale orange color makes it a natural choice for fall.

Serves 6.

1/4 cup butter or margarine
1 pound all-purpose potatoes, diced
2 medium celery stalks, diced
1 large onion, diced
1 teaspoon paprika
2 cups milk
One 13¾-ounce can chicken broth
1 cup water
1 teaspoon salt
1/4 teaspoon freshly ground black pepper
One 10-ounce package shredded extra-sharp Cheddar cheese

In a 4-quart saucepan over medium heat, melt the butter, and in it cook the potatoes, celery, and onion about 10 minutes, or until the vegetables are tender. Add the paprika; cook 1 minute, stirring constantly.

Add the milk, chicken broth, water, salt, and pepper. Bring to a boil over high heat. Reduce the heat to low; cover and simmer 20 minutes. Remove from heat; stir in the Cheddar cheese until melted.

In a food processor or blender, purée the mixture in batches until smooth. Reheat to serve.

RED BLISS POTATO AND OYSTER CHOWDER

There are few dishes quite so appealing as a hearty chowder. Red Bliss potatoes add a flavorful dimension to this recipe.

Serves 6.

¼ cup butter or margarine
1 large onion, diced
1 large garlic clove, minced
2 tablespoons all-purpose flour
2 cups milk
1 pound Red Bliss potatoes, cut into ½-inch cubes
Two 8-ounce cans oysters, with their liquid*
One 10-ounce can clam juice
¾ teaspoon salt
¼ teaspoon freshly ground black pepper
¼ teaspoon hot pepper sauce
Oyster crackers

In a 5-quart saucepan or Dutch oven over medium heat, melt the butter, and in it cook the onion until tender, about 5 minutes, stirring occasionally. Add the garlic; cook 1 minute, stirring frequently.

Add the flour; cook until the mixture thickens slightly. Gradually add the milk until smooth. Stir in the potatoes, the oysters with their liquid, the clam juice, salt, pepper, and hot pepper sauce.

Bring to a boil over high heat. Reduce the heat to low; cover and simmer 20 minutes, or until the potatoes are tender, stirring occasionally. Serve with oyster crackers.

*Substitute 1 pound freshly shucked oysters or fresh or canned clams.

BLACK BEAN AND POTATO SOUP

Here's a robust, nutritionally rich soup to warm the heart and soul, as well as the body.

Serves 8.

One 8-ounce package sliced bacon, diced
1 pound all-purpose potatoes, peeled and diced
2 large carrots, peeled and diced
1 large onion, diced
1 large garlic clove, crushed
4 cups water
One 15-ounce can black beans, drained and rinsed
1 bay leaf
1 beef bouillon cube or envelope
1½ teaspoons salt
1 teaspoon dried oregano leaves
¼ teaspoon freshly ground black pepper

In a 4-quart saucepan oven medium heat, cook the bacon until crisp, about 5 minutes, stirring occasionally. With a slotted spoon, remove the bacon to paper towels to drain.

In the drippings remaining in the saucepan, over medium heat, cook the potatoes, carrots, and onion until the vegetables are tender, stirring occasionally. Add the garlic; cook 1 minute.

Add the water, black beans, bay leaf, beef bouillon, salt, oregano, pepper, and bacon. Bring to a boil over high heat. Reduce the heat to low; cover and simmer 20 minutes, or until the vegetables are tender. Skim off any fat on the surface. Remove the bay leaf.

Purée of Potato and Carrot Soup

This nourishing winter combination takes all of 25 minutes to make, at the outside, and makes thrifty use of everyday kitchen staples. The taste, though, is anything but common.

Serves 6.

1 tablespoon butter or margarine
1 tablespoon vegetable oil
5 medium carrots, peeled and sliced
2 medium all-purpose potatoes, chopped
1 medium onion, sliced
1 large garlic clove, crushed
Two 13¾-ounce cans chicken broth
1½ cups water
1¼ teaspoons salt
¼ teaspoon freshly ground black pepper
1 cup milk
¼ cup chopped parsley

In a 12-inch skillet over medium heat, melt the butter with the oil; and in it cook the carrots, potatoes, and onion for 15 minutes, stirring occasionally. Add the garlic; cook 1 minute longer.

Add the chicken broth, water, salt, and pepper. Bring to a boil over high heat. Reduce the heat to low; simmer 5 minutes, stirring occasionally.

In a blender or food processor, purée the mixture. Return to the saucepan. Add the milk, and heat through. Stir in the chopped parsley.

POTATO BEET BORSCHT

The word borscht has come to mean beet soup in this country, but it is really an old Slavic word for beet. Here it's full of diced purple potatoes, beets, and green cabbage. Beet greens add some zip to this ruby red soup.

Serves 6.

¼ cup vegetable oil
1 pound purple potatoes, peeled and diced
1 medium onion, diced
3 cups diced green cabbage
1 large carrot, peeled and diced
1 large bunch beets with tops
3 cups water
One 13¾-ounce can chicken broth
2 tablespoons cider vinegar
1 tablespoon granulated sugar
2½ teaspoons salt
¼ teaspoon freshly ground black pepper
½ cup sour cream

In a 5-quart saucepan over medium heat, heat the oil, and in it cook the potatoes, onion, cabbage and carrot for about 10 minutes, stirring occasionally.

Meanwhile, cut the beet greens from the beets; chop the greens to make 1 cup. Peel the beets and coarsely shred to make 2 cups.

Add the beets, beet greens, water, chicken broth, cider vinegar, sugar, salt, and pepper to the pan. Bring to a boil over high heat. Reduce the heat to low; cover and simmer 20 minutes longer, stirring occasionally. Top each serving with a dollop of sour cream.

COLD POTATO AND CANTALOUPE SOUP

This light, refreshing summery soup is flavored with orange and mint. For a fun touch, serve it in hollowed-out cantaloupe halves.

Serves 4.

1 medium cantaloupe, peeled and seeded
2 cups cooked potato chunks, cooled
1 cup orange juice
½ cup sour cream
2 tablespoons lemon juice
⅛ teaspoon salt
3 tablespoons grated orange peel
¼ cup orange-flavored liqueur (optional)
Mint sprigs for garnish

Cut the cantaloupe into chunks to make 4 cups. In food processor or blender, purée the cantaloupe, potato chunks, orange juice, sour cream, lemon juice, and salt until smooth.

Transfer to a bowl and stir in the grated orange peel and orange-flavored liqueur, if desired. Cover and refrigerate until well chilled. To serve, garnish with mint sprigs.

CHAPTER THREE

SALADS

Potato Caesar Salad

Warm Shrimp and Potato Salad

Red Potato Salad Niçoise

Red, White, and Blue Potato Salad

Warm Sweet Potato and Turkey Salad

Dill Pesto Potatoes

Roasted Potato, Artichoke, and Tomato Salad

Cajun-Style Sweet Potato and Ham Toss

Hearty Potato and Kielbasa Salad

Warm Mussel and Potato Salad

Asparagus and Potato Salad with Lemon Vinaigrette

Red Bliss Potato, Fennel, and Olive Salad

Potato Tabbouleh

Picnic Potato and Egg Salad

Warm Potato Salad with Bacon

Sautéed Potato and Leek Salad with Champagne Vinaigrette

New Potato and Parsley Salad with Mustard Dressing

Farmer's Market Salad

Roasted Potatoes and Red Peppers with Cumin Dressing

Herbed Potato and Tuna Salad

POTATO CAESAR SALAD

The Caesar is one of the original great salads and an American favorite. The potatoes accentuate the zesty flavor of this dressing.

Serves 6.

2 pounds red potatoes, cut into 1-inch chunks
2 tablespoons lemon juice
1 tablespoon anchovy paste, or 2 anchovies
1 tablespoon grated Parmesan cheese
1 tablespoon Dijon mustard
1 large garlic clove, crushed
¼ teaspoon freshly ground black pepper
⅓ cup olive oil
2 tablespoons chopped parsley
Romaine lettuce leaves

Place the potatoes and enough water to cover in a 2-quart saucepan over high heat and bring to a boil. Reduce the heat to low; cover and simmer 20 minutes, or until the potatoes are tender. Drain.

Meanwhile, in a food processor or blender, blend the lemon juice, anchovy paste, Parmesan cheese, mustard, garlic, and pepper until well blended. Gradually add the olive oil until the mixture is smooth.

Toss the potatoes with the dressing and the parsley. To serve, arrange on lettuce leaves.

WARM SHRIMP AND POTATO SALAD

This elegant salad can be served as an appetizer or a main dish. The success of this recipe depends upon firm potato slices. If overcooked, they will fall apart.

Serves 4.

1 pound Yukon gold potatoes, cut into
*   ¼-inch-thick slices*
1 tablespoon butter or margarine
2 large shallots, finely chopped (about ¼ cup)
1 pound large shrimp, peeled and deveined
2 tablespoons chopped parsley
2 tablespoons white wine vinegar
2 tablespoons olive oil
1 teaspoon prepared horseradish
¾ teaspoon salt
¼ teaspoon freshly ground black pepper
Assorted salad greens

Place the potatoes and enough water to cover in a 2-quart saucepan over high heat and bring to a boil. Reduce the heat to low; cover and simmer 15 minutes, or until the potatoes are just tender. Drain.

Meanwhile, in a 10-inch skillet over medium heat, melt the butter, and in it cook the shallots about 5 minutes. Add the shrimp; cook 3 to 5 minutes, stirring occasionally.

In a large bowl, toss the potatoes, shrimp mixture, parsley, vinegar, olive oil, horseradish, salt, and pepper, and mix well. Serve immediately on assorted salad greens.

RED POTATO SALAD NIÇOISE

A complete meal in itself, this salad goes nicely with a glass of white wine. A baguette and sweet butter enhance the French theme.

Serves 8.

1 pound small red potatoes, cut into quarters
½ pound green beans, cut into 2-inch pieces
3 cups shredded Romaine lettuce
4 hard-cooked eggs, cut into quarters
3 plum tomatoes, cut into wedges
One 6½-ounce can tuna, drained and flaked
1 small red onion, thinly sliced
½ cup oil-cured black olives
Anchovies for garnish (optional)
2 tablespoons Dijon mustard
2 tablespoons white wine vinegar
2 tablespoons small capers
¼ teaspoon freshly ground black pepper
¼ cup extra-virgin olive oil

Place the potatoes and enough water to cover in a 2-quart saucepan over high heat and bring to a boil. Reduce the heat to low; cover and simmer 12 minutes. Add the green beans; simmer 3 minutes longer, or until the vegetables are tender. Drain.

On a large platter, place the shredded lettuce. Arrange the potato quarters, green beans, eggs, tomatoes, tuna, onion, olives, and anchovies, if desired.

In a small bowl, stir together the Dijon mustard, vinegar, capers, and pepper. Gradually add the olive oil until completely blended and smooth.

To serve, toss the salad with the dressing.

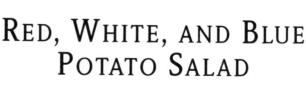

RED, WHITE, AND BLUE
POTATO SALAD

Red potatoes, all-purpose potatoes, and purple potatoes are the flavorful trio that make up this colorful, festive salad. It's a perfect choice for the Fourth of July or other family get-togethers.

Serves 8.

1 pound red potatoes, cut into 1-inch chunks
1 pound all-purpose potatoes, peeled and cut into
  1-inch chunks
1 pound purple potatoes, peeled and cut into 1-inch chunks
1 small red onion, minced
⅓ cup sour cream
¼ cup chopped chives
2 tablespoons prepared horseradish
2 tablespoons mayonnaise
1 tablespoon white wine vinegar
1½ teaspoons salt
¼ teaspoon freshly ground black pepper
Red cabbage leaves

Place all the potatoes and enough water to cover in a 4-quart saucepan over high heat, and bring to a boil. Reduce the heat to low; cover and simmer 20 minutes, or until the potatoes are tender. Drain.

Meanwhile, in a large bowl, combine the onion, sour cream, chives, horseradish, mayonnaise, vinegar, salt, and pepper. Add the potatoes; toss to mix well. Refrigerate until ready to serve.

To serve, line a large platter with cabbage leaves; top with potato salad.

WARM SWEET POTATO AND TURKEY SALAD

Sweet potatoes gain a whole new personality when combined with chutney and tart balsamic vinegar. This is a great way to use up left-over turkey.

Serves 4.

1 pound sweet potatoes, peeled and cut into 1-inch chunks
2 tablespoons olive oil
1 pound turkey breast, cut into 1-inch chunks
1 teaspoon salt
½ cup chopped mango chutney
¼ cup chopped parsley
1 tablespoon balsamic vinegar
¼ teaspoon freshly ground black pepper
Lettuce leaves

Place the sweet potato chunks and enough water to cover in a 2-quart saucepan over high heat, and bring to a boil. Reduce the heat to low; cover and simmer 10 minutes, or until the potato chunks are tender. Drain.

Meanwhile, in a 12-inch skillet over medium-high heat, heat the oil until hot, and in it cook the turkey chunks with ½ teaspoon salt about 5 minutes, until browned, stirring frequently. Add the sweet potatoes, chutney, parsley, balsamic vinegar, pepper, and the remaining ½ tea-spoon salt. Cook 1 to 2 minutes, stirring frequently to blend the flavors. Serve the salad warm on a bed of lettuce leaves.

DILL PESTO POTATOES

Serve this salad with grilled fish or poultry. The pesto, redolent with dill, never tasted so good!

Serves 6.

1 pound red potatoes, cut into 1-inch chunks
¾ cup loosely packed fresh dill
½ cup loosely packed parsley
½ cup pecans or walnuts
¼ cup olive oil
3 tablespoons grated Parmesan cheese
2 large garlic cloves
½ teaspoon salt
¼ teaspoon freshly ground black pepper
1 pint cherry tomatoes, each cut in half
¾ pound yellow squash, cut into ¼-inch slices

Place the potatoes and enough water to cover in a 2-quart saucepan over high heat, and bring to a boil. Reduce the heat to low; cover and simmer 15 minutes, or until the potatoes are tender. Drain.

In a blender or food processor, blend the dill, parsley, nuts, oil, Parmesan cheese, garlic, salt, and pepper until the dill pesto is well blended.

In a large bowl, toss the potatoes, tomatoes, and squash, and dress with the pesto.

ROASTED POTATO, ARTICHOKE, AND TOMATO SALAD

Roasted vegetables cooked with herbs have intense and complex flavors. Toss them in oil, garlic, and rosemary, then simply bake. This dish is particularly delicious served warm, on a bed of leaf lettuce.

Serves 4 to 6.

1½ *pounds all-purpose potatoes, cut into 1½-inch chunks*
¼ *cup olive oil*
4 large garlic cloves, sliced
1½ *teaspoons chopped fresh rosemary, or ½ teaspoon*
    dried rosemary
½ *teaspoon salt*
¼ *teaspoon freshly ground black pepper*
One 9-ounce package frozen artichoke hearts, thawed
4 plum tomatoes, cut into 1½-inch chunks

Preheat the oven to 400° F. In a 13-×9-inch baking pan, toss the potatoes, oil, garlic, rosemary, salt, and pepper. Roast 20 minutes.

Remove the baking pan from the oven. Add the artichoke hearts and tomato chunks; toss to mix well. Roast 20 minutes longer, or until the vegetables are tender, stirring occasionally. Serve warm.

Cajun-Style Sweet Potato and Ham Toss

Don't be shy with sweet potatoes—they're incredibly versatile! Here they are sautéed, mixed with ham and spices, and dressed, as for a salad. This dish travels especially well and is a good choice for picnics or pot luck suppers.

Serves 4.

1½ pounds sweet potatoes, peeled and cut into ¾-inch chunks
2 tablespoons olive oil
½ pound boiled ham, cut into ½-inch chunks
3 large scallions, sliced
1 large garlic clove, crushed
¼ teaspoon freshly ground black pepper
1 tablespoon Dijon mustard
1 tablespoon cider vinegar
½ teaspoon cayenne pepper
¼ teaspoon salt
Watercress sprigs

Place the sweet potatoes and enough water to cover in a 3-quart saucepan over high heat and bring to a boil. Reduce the heat to low; cover and simmer 10 to 15 minutes, or until the potatoes are just tender. Drain.

In a 12-inch skillet over medium heat, heat 1 tablespoon olive oil, and in it cook the ham chunks, scallions, garlic, and black pepper until the ham is lightly browned, stirring occasionally. Add the sweet potato chunks; cook 3 to 5 minutes longer, or until tender.

In a large bowl, combine the mustard, vinegar, cayenne pepper, and salt. Add the sweet potato mixture; toss to mix well.

To serve, arrange the watercress sprigs on a platter; top with the sweet potato salad.

HEARTY POTATO AND KIELBASA SALAD

The strong accents of kielbasa sausage and leeks make for a substantial salad. Serve it as a simple first course or as a complete lunch in itself. Apples or pears follow nicely as dessert.

Serves 6.

¼ cup vegetable oil
1 pound Yukon gold potatoes, peeled and cut into ¼-inch
*   slices*
1 pound kielbasa, cut into ¼-inch slices
1 large leek, thinly sliced
1 tablespoon red wine vinegar
½ teaspoon salt
¼ teaspoon freshly ground black pepper

In a 12-inch skillet over medium heat, heat the oil, and in it cook the potatoes until tender, turning occasionally, 10 to 15 minutes. With a slotted spoon, remove to plate.

In the oil remaining in the skillet over medium-high heat, cook the kielbasa and leek, about 3 minutes, stirring occasionally. Return the potatoes to the skillet. Add the vinegar, salt, and pepper; toss to mix well. Serve warm or refrigerate to serve later.

WARM MUSSEL AND POTATO SALAD

Fresh mussels are relatively affordable in comparison to other shell-fish, and their burst of flavor goes a long way. Here potatoes act as their foil, for a flavorful duet.

Serves 4.

> 1 pound all-purpose potatoes, peeled and cut into
>   ¼-inch-thick slices
> 2 dozen large mussels
> ¼ cup dry white wine
> 2 tablespoons olive oil
> 2 tablespoons minced red onion
> 1 tablespoon white wine vinegar
> ¼ cup chopped parsley
> 1 teaspoon salt
> 2 plum tomatoes, diced

Place the potatoes and enough water to cover in a 3-quart sauce-pan over high heat, and bring to a boil. Reduce the heat to low; cover and simmer until just tender, 10 to 15 minutes. Do not overcook. Drain.

Meanwhile, rinse the mussels in running cold water; discard any with open shells. Pull off their beards and place the mussels in a 2-quart saucepan with the white wine. Over medium heat, bring to a boil. Cover and simmer 5 to 10 minutes until all the shells open. With a slotted spoon, remove the mussels from the shells and place in a bowl. Discard any unopened mussels. Discard the shells. Rinse the mussels in cooking broth to remove any sand.

In a large bowl, combine the olive oil, onion, vinegar, parsley, and salt. Gently stir in the potato slices, the warm mussels, and the toma-toes; toss to mix well.

CHAPTER THREE

Asparagus and Potato Salad with Lemon Vinaigrette

This is a wonderful salad for dining al fresco in the spring, summer, or early fall. Serve with poached or sautéed fish or chicken.

Serves 4.

1 pound red potatoes, cut into 1-inch chunks
1 small bunch asparagus (about ½ pound), cut into
* 2-inch pieces*
2 tablespoons extra-virgin olive oil
2 tablespoons lemon juice
1 tablespoon grated lemon peel
1 garlic clove, minced
½ teaspoon salt

Place the potatoes and enough water to cover in a 2-quart saucepan over high heat, and bring to a boil. Reduce the heat to low; cover and simmer 15 minutes, or until the potatoes are almost tender. Add the asparagus; cook 2 minutes longer, or until the vegetables are tender. Drain.

In a large bowl, mix the olive oil, lemon juice, lemon peel, garlic, and salt. Add the potatoes and asparagus; toss to mix well. Serve warm or refrigerate to serve later.

RED BLISS POTATO, FENNEL, AND OLIVE SALAD

The anise accent of fennel and the pungency of garlic give this salad a real kick. On a hot summer day, you might even serve it as a meatless entrée.

Serves 4.

3 tablespoons olive oil
1 pound Red Bliss potatoes, cut into
*   1½-inch chunks*
1 fennel bulb, cut into thin strips
2 large garlic cloves
½ cup small oil-cured black olives
1 tablespoon white wine vinegar
Escarole leaves

In a 12-inch skillet over medium heat, heat the olive oil, and in it cook the potatoes for 10 minutes, stirring occasionally. Add the fennel and garlic; cook 5 to 10 minutes, stirring frequently, until the vegetables are tender. Stir in the olives and vinegar.

To serve, arrange the escarole leaves over a platter and spoon the salad over them.

POTATO TABBOULEH

Everyone loves this refreshing Middle Eastern salad made with bulgur wheat, potatoes, tomatoes, and mint. It's healthy, hearty, and deliciously different with potatoes. The success of this recipe depends upon the supporting cast, not the star.

Serves 6.

1 cup cracked wheat (bulgur)
1 pound red potatoes, cut into ½-inch cubes
3 scallions, sliced thin
1 large tomato, chopped
½ cup chopped parsley
3 tablespoons chopped fresh mint
2 tablespoons freshly squeezed lemon juice
1 tablespoon olive oil
1½ teaspoons salt
½ teaspoon freshly ground black pepper
Romaine lettuce leaves

In a large bowl, cover the cracked wheat with cold water; let stand 1 hour. Drain and squeeze out any excess water.

Meanwhile, place the potatoes and enough water to cover in a 2-quart saucepan and bring to a boil. Reduce the heat to low; cover and simmer 10 minutes, or until the potatoes are tender. Drain.

In a large bowl, combine the scallions, tomato, parsley, mint, lemon juice, olive oil, salt, pepper, potatoes, and cracked wheat. Line a large bowl with Romaine leaves and spoon the salad over the greens.

PICNIC POTATO AND EGG SALAD

Like apple pie and cornbread, potato salad is quintessential American fare. Barbecued ribs, corn on the cob, steaks, and sandwiches of any kind are natural complements.

Serves 8.

3 pounds red potatoes, cut into 1-inch chunks
¼ cup mayonnaise
¼ cup minced dill pickle
2 tablespoons cider vinegar
1 tablespoon Dijon mustard
1½ teaspoons salt
¼ teaspoon cayenne pepper
4 hard-cooked eggs, chopped
3 scallions, sliced
2 celery stalks, sliced
½ cup chopped parsley

Place the potatoes and enough water to cover in a 4-quart saucepan over high heat and bring to a boil. Reduce the heat to low; cover and simmer 20 minutes, or until the potatoes are tender. Drain.

Meanwhile, in a large bowl, combine the mayonnaise, pickle, vinegar, Dijon mustard, salt, and cayenne pepper. Add the potatoes, eggs, scallions, celery, and parsley. Toss to mix well. Refrigerate until ready to serve.

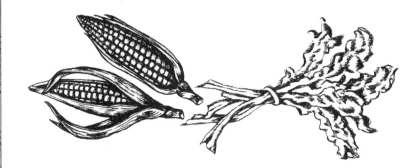

WARM POTATO SALAD
WITH BACON

There are many ways to enjoy this classic German recipe. For a traditional meal, pair it with knockwurst or porkchops and a dark bread. It also makes a spectacular topping for grilled hamburgers.

Serves 4.

1½ pounds Yukon gold (yellow) potatoes, peeled and cut into
  ¾-inch-thick pieces
4 ounces sliced bacon, diced
3 scallions, sliced
1 tablespoon all-purpose flour
2 tablespoons red wine vinegar
½ teaspoon salt
⅛ teaspoon freshly ground black pepper
1 tablespoon chopped parsley
Lettuce leaves

Place the potatoes and enough water to cover in a 2-quart saucepan over high heat and bring to a boil. Reduce the heat to low; cover and simmer 15 minutes, or until the potatoes are tender. Drain.

Meanwhile, in a 12-inch skillet over medium heat, cook the bacon until crisp, 5 to 10 minutes, stirring occasionally. With a slotted spoon, remove to paper towels to drain.

Remove all but 2 tablespoons of the drippings from the skillet. Add the scallions and flour; cook 1 to 2 minutes, until the mixture thickens, stirring frequently.

Add the vinegar, potatoes, bacon, salt, and pepper. Heat through. Stir in the chopped parsley. Immediately spoon the salad onto a platter lined with lettuce leaves.

SAUTÉED POTATO AND LEEK SALAD WITH CHAMPAGNE VINAIGRETTE

Here is a salad with Gallic roots. If you are unable to find champagne vinegar, try a good white wine vinegar.

Serves 4.

3 tablespoons olive oil
1 pound red potatoes, cut into ¼-inch-thick slices
2 large leeks, thinly sliced
¾ teaspoon salt
3 tablespoons champagne vinegar or white wine vinegar
1 tablespoon chopped parsley

In a 12-inch skillet over medium heat, heat 2 tablespoons of the oil, and in it cook the potatoes about 10 minutes, stirring occasionally. Add the leeks and salt; cook 3 minutes longer, or until the potatoes and leeks are tender.

In a large bowl, combine the vinegar, parsley, and the remaining 1 tablespoon oil. Add the potato mixture; toss to mix well. Serve warm or refrigerate to serve later.

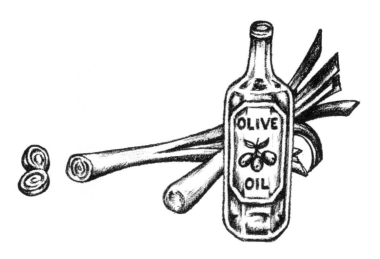

New Potato and Parsley Salad with Mustard Dressing

A good choice for summer dining, this salad is delicious with marinated grilled flank steak or fish.

Serves 6.

2 pounds new potatoes, cut into chunks
¼ cup Dijon mustard
¼ cup cider vinegar
2 large garlic cloves, crushed
½ teaspoon salt
¼ teaspoon freshly ground black pepper
⅓ cup olive oil
¼ cup chopped parsley
Lettuce leaves

Place the potatoes and enough water to cover in a 2-quart saucepan over high heat and bring to a boil. Reduce the heat to low. Cover and simmer 10 minutes, or until the potatoes are tender. Drain.

Meanwhile, in a large bowl, combine the Dijon mustard, vinegar, garlic, salt, and pepper. Gradually add the olive oil until the dressing is well blended.

FARMER'S MARKET SALAD

This chunky salad includes a variety of fresh vegetables and is tossed in a light yogurt dressing.

Serves 6.

1½ pounds red potatoes, cut into 1-inch chunks
2 cups fresh corn (from 2 large ears)
1 medium bunch broccoli, cut into 2- × ½-inch pieces
¾ cup plain yogurt
2 tablespoons olive oil
1 tablespoon white wine vinegar
2 teaspoons chopped fresh thyme
1 teaspoon salt
¼ teaspoon freshly ground black pepper
1 large red bell pepper, seeded and cut into thin strips

In a 4-quart saucepan over high heat, heat the potatoes and 3 quarts water and bring to a boil. Reduce the heat to low; cover and simmer 10 minutes. Add the corn; simmer 5 minutes. Add the broccoli; simmer 2 minutes longer, or until the vegetables are fork-tender. Drain. Rinse in running cold water.

In a large bowl, combine the yogurt, oil, vinegar, thyme, salt, and pepper until well mixed. Add the reserved vegetables and red pepper strips; toss to mix well. Serve at room temperature or refrigerate to serve later.

Roasted Potatoes and Red Peppers with Cumin Dressing

Cumin seeds give this impressive yet easy-to-make salad its distinctive, pleasing flavor.

Serves 4 to 6.

1½ pounds red potatoes, cut into ¼-inch-thick slices
2 medium red bell peppers, cut into ¼-inch thick slices
¼ cup cider vinegar
3 tablespoons vegetable oil
1½ teaspoons cumin seeds
1 large garlic clove, crushed
½ teaspoon salt
¼ teaspoon freshly ground black pepper
Boston lettuce leaves

Preheat the oven to 450° F. In an 11-×9-inch baking pan, combine the potatoes and red peppers. In a small bowl, combine the vinegar, oil, cumin seeds, garlic, salt, and pepper. Toss the mixture with the potatoes in the baking pan.

Bake 25 to 30 minutes, until the potatoes and peppers are tender, turning occasionally. Serve over lettuce leaves.

HERBED POTATO AND
TUNA SALAD

Your dinner or lunch guests will love this light and lovely potato and tuna salad, complemented by Tomato-Caper Salsa. If fresh tuna is not available, use canned tuna. In warm weather, consider grilling the potatoes and tuna outdoors.

Serves 4 to 6.

1 pound Yukon gold potatoes
One 16-ounce tuna steak, about ¾-inch-thick*
¼ cup olive oil
1 teaspoon salt
2 tablespoons chopped fresh rosemary, or 2 teaspoons dried
  rosemary
½ teaspoon freshly ground black pepper

TOMATO-CAPER SALSA

4 medium tomatoes, chopped
¼ cup capers, drained
½ cup chopped black olives
2 tablespoons lemon juice
2 tablespoons olive oil

Preheat the broiler. Cut the potatoes into ½-inch-thick wedges; arrange on a large cookie sheet with the fresh tuna steak.

In a small bowl, combine the olive oil, salt, rosemary, and pepper. Brush the mixture over the potatoes and tuna. Broil for 10 minutes, turning once and brushing occasionally with the oil mixture.

Meanwhile, in another bowl, toss together the tomatoes, capers, black olives, lemon juice, and olive oil. Arrange the potatoes and tuna on a large platter. Serve with the Tomato-Caper Salsa.

*Substitute two 6½-ounce cans tuna, drained and flaked, for fresh tuna. Do not broil.

CHAPTER FOUR

MAIN COURSES

Anchovy Potato Pizza

Potato and Lentil Curry

Three-Cheese Potato Soufflé

Mushroom-Filled Potato Pancakes

Potato and Chorizo Frittata

Basil Gnocchi with Fresh Tomato Salsa

Potato and Sausage Lasagna

Potato and Cabbage Pirogies

Baked Potatoes with Assorted Toppings

Vegetable Pot Pies with Mashed Potato Crust

Potato and Onion Tortilla

Potato Moussaka

Moroccan-Style Potato and Veal Stew

Sausage, Potatoes, and Peppers

Pasta with Potatoes and Spicy Sausages

Seafood Potato Gumbo

Potato Chili

ANCHOVY POTATO PIZZA

Here is an easy-to-make dough that is first spread with anchovy oil, then topped with sliced red potatoes. Top with olives if anchovies don't appeal to you.

Serves 8.

DOUGH

1½ cups all-purpose flour
1 cup mashed potatoes
3 tablespoons olive oil
1 teaspoon salt

TOPPING

3 tablespoons olive oil
1 tablespoon minced anchovies
1 pound red potatoes, very thinly sliced
2 tablespoons chopped parsley

In a medium bowl, combine the flour, mashed potatoes, olive oil, and salt. Using your hands, knead the mixture until the dough forms a ball. Let rest 5 minutes.

Preheat the oven to 400° F. Press the dough into a 12-inch pizza pan. In a small cup, stir together the olive oil and the anchovies. Brush some anchovy oil over the dough. Arrange the sliced potatoes over the dough. Brush with the remaining anchovy oil. Bake, preferably on the bottom rack of oven, about 20 minutes, or until the potatoes are tender and the crust is crisp. Garnish with parsley.

POTATO AND LENTIL CURRY

This vegetarian dish resonates with the flavors of India. If you have a recipe for making your own curry powder, by all means use it here.

Serves 6.

>*3 tablespoons olive oil*
>*1 large onion, diced*
>*1 large garlic clove, crushed*
>*1 tablespoon curry powder*
>*1 cup brown lentils*
>*One 13¾-ounce can chicken broth*
>*1 pound all-purpose potatoes, cut into 1-inch chunks*
>*3 large carrots, peeled and diced*
>*1 teaspoon salt*
>*1½ cups water*
>*1 cup broccoli florets*

In a 4-quart saucepan over medium heat, heat the olive oil, and in it cook the onion about 5 minutes, stirring occasionally. Add the garlic and curry powder; cook about 1 minute, stirring frequently.

Add the lentils, chicken broth, potatoes, carrots, salt, and water, and bring to a boil over high heat. Reduce the heat to low; cover and simmer 25 minutes, stirring occasionally.

Add the broccoli; simmer 5 minutes longer, or until the vegetables and lentils are tender.

THREE-CHEESE
POTATO SOUFFLÉ

The base of this soufflé is made not from the customary milk, flour, and egg combination but from a blend of mashed potatoes, egg yolks, and milk. The stiffly beaten egg whites still work their magic, though— so serve this immediately, as it comes out of the oven.

Serves 6.

4 small baking potatoes, peeled and cut into chunks
¾ cup milk
¾ cup shredded sharp Cheddar cheese
½ cup shredded Swiss cheese
¼ cup grated Parmesan cheese
3 large scallions, sliced
1 teaspoon salt
¼ teaspoon freshly ground black pepper
3 large eggs, separated

Place the potato chunks and enough water to cover in a 3-quart saucepan over high heat and bring to a boil. Reduce the heat to low; cover and simmer 15 minutes, or until the potatoes are tender. Drain. Cool slightly.

In a large bowl with the mixer on low speed, beat the potatoes until smooth. Add the milk, Cheddar, Swiss, and Parmesan cheeses, scallions, salt, pepper, and egg yolks; beat on low speed until the ingredients are well mixed.

Preheat the oven to 375° F. In a small bowl with the mixer on high speed, beat the egg whites until stiff peaks form. Gently fold the beaten egg whites into the potato mixture. Spoon the mixture into a greased 2-quart soufflé dish. Bake about 50 minutes, or until the soufflé is puffed and golden.

MUSHROOM-FILLED POTATO PANCAKES

Each pancake contains a delicious surprise—sliced mushrooms. Serve these as a main dish with chutney or applesauce, or make them smaller to serve as accompaniments to grilled or roasted meats.

Serves 4.

2 pounds Yukon gold potatoes, peeled
1 large egg, beaten
3 tablespoons all-purpose flour
2 tablespoons snipped fresh chives
½ teaspoon salt
¼ teaspoon freshly ground black pepper
1 tablespoon butter or margarine
1 tablespoon vegetable oil
4 medium mushrooms, sliced (about ¾ cup)

Coarsely grate the potatoes. In a large bowl, combine the potatoes, egg, flour, chives, salt, and pepper until they are well mixed.

In a 12-inch skillet over medium heat, heat the butter and oil until hot. Spoon ¼ cupful of the potato mixture into the skillet. Quickly spread the mixture into a 4-inch round; arrange some sliced mushrooms over the potato mixture; top with ¼ cupful of the potato mixture, sealing the edges with a fork. Repeat with the remaining potato mixture and mushrooms to make 4 pancakes in all.

Cook the pancakes about 4 minutes on each side, or until golden and crisp, turning once. Serve immediately.

POTATO AND CHORIZO FRITTATA

If you can't find chorizo in the market, use salami, Taylor ham, or Canadian bacon. This frittata is a winner as an appetizer (cut into squares) or as picnic fare. Serve it warm or at room temperature.

Serves 6.

1 large yellow potato, cut into ½-inch cubes
2 tablespoons olive oil
4 ounces chorizo sausage or salami, cut into ½-inch cubes
½ teaspoon salt
4 large eggs
¼ teaspoon freshly ground black pepper
¼ cup shredded mozzarella cheese
1 tablespoon chopped parsley

Place the potato cubes and enough water to cover in a small saucepan over high heat and bring to a boil. Reduce the heat to low; cover and simmer 5 to 10 minutes, or until the potatoes are tender. Drain well.

In a 10-inch ovenproof skillet over medium heat, heat 1 tablespoon of the olive oil, and in it cook the potato and chorizo with the salt for 3 to 4 minutes until browned, stirring frequently. Remove to a bowl.

Preheat the broiler. In the same skillet over medium-low heat, heat the remaining 1 tablespoon olive oil. Beat the eggs with the pepper; add to the skillet. Cook, stirring lightly, until the bottom is set, about 3 to 4 minutes. (The top will still be wet.)

Add the potato mixture to the eggs; sprinkle with the mozzarella cheese. Place the skillet under the broiler; cook about 2 minutes, or until the frittata is golden and sizzling. Sprinkle with parsley. Cut into wedges and serve.

BASIL GNOCCHI WITH FRESH TOMATO SALSA

Gnocchi are dumplings, usually made with a potato-based dough. They derive from Italy, where they are served as a first course, often dusted with grated cheese or cleverly sauced. These depend heavily on the splendid flavor of basil, which is in the dough and in the refreshing tomato sauce that serves as a topping. They take some time to make, but the effort is well worth it.

Serves 8.

BASIL GNOCCHI

3 large baking potatoes, peeled
2 cups all-purpose flour
1 large egg
1 cup chopped fresh basil
1 teaspoon salt

FRESH TOMATO SALSA

2 tablespoons olive oil
1 large onion, diced
4 medium tomatoes, chopped
1 cup chopped fresh basil
1 large garlic clove, crushed
1½ teaspoons salt
¼ teaspoon freshly ground black pepper

Grated Parmesan cheese

Place the potatoes and enough water to cover in a 2-quart saucepan over high heat and bring to a boil. Reduce the heat to low; cover and simmer about 25 minutes, or until the potatoes are tender. Drain. Cool the potatoes completely.

In a large bowl, mash the potatoes well (or use a ricer). Stir in the flour, egg, basil, and salt. Knead the mixture about 5 minutes, adding more flour if necessary. The dough should be a bit sticky on the inside.

Do not overwork the dough, or it will require more flour, making the *gnocchi* heavy.

Cut the dough into 12 equal pieces. On a lightly floured surface, with floured hands, roll each piece of dough into a ½-inch-thick rope; cut the rope into ½-inch pieces. Repeat with the remaining dough and flour. Set aside.

To prepare the salsa: In a 12-inch skillet over medium heat, heat the olive oil, and in it cook the onion about 5 minutes, or until tender, stirring occasionally. Add the tomatoes, basil, garlic, salt, and pepper; bring to a boil over high heat. Reduce the heat to low; simmer, uncovered, 5 to 10 minutes, until the liquid is absorbed, stirring occasionally. Keep warm.

In a 5-quart saucepan, bring 3 quarts salted water to a boil. Add the *gnocchi*, stirring constantly. Boil 2 to 3 minutes until the *gnocchi* float to the top. Drain. Toss with the Fresh Tomato Salsa and serve with grated Parmesan cheese.

POTATO AND
SAUSAGE LASAGNA

Potato and sausage lasagna is a perfect dish for family dinners. Children may prefer sweet Italian sausage instead of hot. Serve with a tossed green salad and a good loaf of bread.

Serves 8.

4 large baking potatoes, peeled and cut into
  ¼-inch-thick slices
1 pound hot or sweet Italian sausages
One 14-ounce jar spaghetti sauce
One 15-ounce container ricotta cheese
2 tablespoons chopped parsley
One 8-ounce package shredded mozzarella

Place the potatoes and enough water to cover in a 3-quart saucepan over high heat and bring to a boil. Reduce the heat to low; cover and simmer 10 to 15 minutes, until just tender. Drain.

Meanwhile, remove the sausages from their casings. In a 12-inch skillet over medium heat, cook the sausages until well browned, about 10 minutes, stirring occasionally. Carefully drain off the fat. Stir in the spaghetti sauce.

Preheat the oven to 375° F. In a medium bowl, together stir the ricotta cheese and chopped parsley. In a 12-×8-inch baking dish, arrange half of the potatoes in a single layer. Top with half of the sausage mixture, half of the ricotta mixture, and half of the mozzarella cheese; repeat with the remaining ingredients.

Cover the baking dish with foil. Bake 30 minutes. Remove foil; bake 15 minutes longer, or until the mixture is hot and bubbly.

POTATO AND
CABBAGE PIROGIES

Pirogies, a filling main course, can also be served in smaller portions as starters. This is a great dish to have in your repertoire.

Serves 6.

¼ cup butter or margarine
3 cups chopped green cabbage
1 medium onion, diced
1 cup mashed potatoes
1½ teaspoons salt
2¼ cups all-purpose flour
1 large egg
¾ cup water
¾ cup milk
¼ cup chopped parsley
¼ teaspoon freshly ground white pepper

In a 10-inch skillet over medium heat, melt the butter, and in it cook the cabbage and onion until tender, about 10 minutes, stirring occasionally. Stir in the mashed potatoes and ½ teaspoon of the salt.

To prepare the dough: In a large bowl, stir the flour, egg, water, and the remaining 1 teaspoon salt. Knead the dough until it does not fall apart or stick to your fingers.

On a lightly floured surface, roll out the dough ⅛ inch thick. Cut the dough into 2-inch rounds. Spoon 1 teaspoonful of the potato filling into the center of a round; brush the edges with water; top with another round and pinch the edges together to seal completely. Repeat with the remaining dough and filling. You will have leftover filling; reserve.

In a 4-quart saucepan, bring 3 inches of water to a boil. Meanwhile, in a blender or food processor, blend the reserved filling and milk until smooth. In a small saucepan over low heat, heat the potato mixture until hot. Stir in the parsley and pepper; keep warm. Add the pirogies to the boiling water. Boil 2 to 3 minutes. Drain. Toss with the sauce and serve at once.

BAKED POTATOES WITH ASSORTED TOPPINGS

For a fun "potato buffet" party, place assorted toppings in serving bowls and let guests help themselves. There is a good selection from which to choose below, but let your imagination be your best guide.

Serves 6.

6 large baking potatoes
Vegetable oil

Preheat the oven to 450° F. Scrub the potatoes to remove any dirt. Dry the potatoes and prick with a fork. Rub the skins lightly with the vegetable oil. Place the potatoes on a cookie sheet or jelly-roll pan.

Bake potatoes 45 minutes, or until tender. Split the potatoes and press with your fingertips to loosen the pulp.

Serve with one or more of the following toppings.

ASSORTED TOPPINGS

AMERICAN: Shredded American cheese, bacon bits, and cooked broccoli

ITALIAN: Pesto sauce and shredded mozzarella cheese

MEXICAN: Spicy salsa, jalapeño pepper rings, and shredded Monterey Jack; *or* guacamole and crumbled taco chips

FRENCH: Sautéed mushrooms and Brie, Roquefort, or goat cheese

RUSSIAN: Sour cream and black or red caviar

GREEK: Crumbled feta cheese, sliced scallions, and Greek olives

BRAZILIAN: Canned black beans and chunky salsa

ORIENTAL: Sautéed *shiitake* mushrooms and bean sprouts

SPANISH: Chopped green or black olives and cooked chorizo sausage

CANADIAN: Diced Canadian bacon, scallions, and Cheddar cheese chunks

SICILIAN: Chopped pepperoni, pizza sauce, and grated Parmesan cheese

GERMAN: Sauerkraut, caraway seeds, and diced red apple

HAWAIIAN: Chopped ham and pineapple chunks

NIÇOISE: Flaked tuna, green bean pieces, diced red onion, and tomato

HERBED: Minced chopped fresh parsley, basil, oregano, thyme, or dill

VEGETARIAN: Mixed cooked vegetables

DIET: Dollop of yogurt and snipped chives

CHILDREN'S: Sliced frankfurters and cheese spread

VEGETABLE POT PIES WITH MASHED POTATO CRUST

These tempting vegetable pot pies can be assembled ahead, then frozen. Bake frozen at 450° F. for 1 hour, or until the tops are golden and the mixture is hot and bubbly.

Serves 4.

FILLING

¼ cup olive oil
1 pound all-purpose potatoes, peeled and diced
2 large carrots, peeled and thinly sliced
4 ounces mushrooms, sliced
4 ounces green beans, cut into 1-inch pieces
2 large celery stalks, chopped
¼ cup all-purpose flour
1 cup milk
One 13¾-ounce can chicken broth
1 teaspoon salt
½ teaspoon dried tarragon
¼ teaspoon ground white pepper

POTATO TOPPING

2 cups mashed potatoes
2 tablespoons butter or margarine
1 large egg
2 tablespoons chopped parsley

In a 3-quart saucepan over medium heat, heat the olive oil, and in it cook the potatoes, carrots, mushrooms, green beans, and celery until tender, stirring occasionally.

Mix the flour and milk in a measuring cup. Stir into the saucepan along with the chicken broth, salt, tarragon, and pepper. Bring to a boil over high heat. Reduce the heat to low; cover and simmer 15 minutes, or until the vegetables are tender.

Spoon the vegetable mixture into four 2-cup aluminum pie plates, or other ovenproof casseroles or containers. Preheat the oven to 425° F.

In a medium bowl, combine the mashed potatoes, butter, egg, and parsley. Top each container with some of the potato mixture, spreading it evenly to cover the surface. Bake 20 to 25 minutes, or until the tops are golden.

POTATO AND ONION TORTILLA

We all know what the word tortilla means when it is used in a Mexican or Southwestern context. But in Spanish, tortilla means "omelet." Serve this simple, appealing dish for brunch or a light supper, either hot or at room temperature.

Serves 4.

2 tablespoons olive oil
½ pound red potatoes, thinly sliced
1 small red onion, thinly sliced
4 large eggs
1 ounce chive cream cheese, softened
½ teaspoon salt

In a 12-inch skillet over medium heat, heat the oil and in it cook the sliced potatoes and onion until the potatoes are tender, 8 to 10 minutes, stirring frequently.

In a medium bowl, beat the eggs, cream cheese, and salt. Pour over the potato mixture in the skillet. Reduce heat to medium-low, stirring lightly until the mixture is set, about 5 minutes.

To serve, cut the tortilla into wedges. Serve hot or refrigerate to serve later.

POTATO MOUSSAKA

Potatoes are a new twist on moussaka, or eggplant casserole, a classic Greek dish that has many American fans. You can use ground lamb, the traditional meat, instead of beef, if desired. This can be prepared ahead of time and reheated.

Serves 8.

1 pound all-purpose potatoes, thinly sliced

BEEF LAYER

1½ pounds lean ground beef
1 large onion, diced
2 large garlic cloves, minced
2 large tomatoes, chopped
One 8-ounce can tomato sauce
1½ teaspoons salt
¾ teaspoon dried dill

CHEESE SAUCE

½ cup butter or margarine
⅓ cup all-purpose flour
4 cups milk
2 large eggs, slightly beaten
1 cup shredded Kasseri or Kefalotiri cheese
1 teaspoon salt
¼ teaspoon freshly ground black pepper

Place the potatoes and enough water to cover in a 2-quart saucepan over high heat and bring to a boil. Reduce the heat to low; cover and simmer 5 to 10 minutes until potatoes are just tender. Do not overcook. Drain.

In a 12-inch skillet over medium-high heat, cook the ground beef, onion, and garlic until the beef is browned, about 10 minutes, stirring occasionally. Spoon off excess fat. Stir in the tomatoes, tomato sauce, salt, and dill. Bring to a boil over high heat. Reduce the heat to low; cover and simmer 10 minutes to blend flavors, stirring occasionally.

Meanwhile, prepare the sauce: In a 2-quart saucepan over medium heat, melt the butter. Stir in the flour; cook 1 minute, stirring constantly. Gradually stir in the milk. Reduce the heat to low; stir in the eggs. Cook until mixture is smooth and thickened, stirring constantly. Stir in ½ cup of the cheese, the salt, and pepper.

Preheat the oven to 350° F. Into a 13- × 9-inch baking dish spoon one-third cheese sauce. Layer half of the sliced potatoes, half of the meat mixture, and one-third of the cheese sauce. Repeat with the remaining potatoes, meat, and cheese sauce. Sprinkle with the remaining ½ cup grated cheese. Cover the baking dish with foil. Bake 30 minutes. Remove the foil and bake 15 minutes longer, or until the mixture is hot and bubbly. Let stand 10 minutes before serving.

MOROCCAN-STYLE POTATO AND VEAL STEW

Moroccans love to cook with a variety of marvelous spices, and this fragrant stew reflects their diverse culinary repertoire. The addition of couscous—virtually the Moroccan national dish—lends another dimension of texture.

Serves 6.

3 tablespoons vegetable oil
1½ pounds veal or lamb for stew, cut into 1-inch chunks
1 pound all-purpose potatoes, peeled and cut into
  1-inch chunks
1 large onion, diced
½ pound green beans, cut into 2-inch pieces
2 large garlic cloves, crushed
One 28-ounce can crushed tomatoes
2½ cups water
1 bay leaf
2 tablespoons capers
1 teaspoon salt
¼ teaspoon crushed red pepper
⅛ teaspoon ground cloves
One 9-ounce package frozen artichoke hearts
1 cup couscous

In a 4-quart saucepan over medium-high heat, heat 2 tablespoons of the oil, and in it cook the meat about 5 minutes, or until browned on all sides. With a slotted spoon, remove the meat to a bowl.

In the same saucepan, heat the remaining 1 tablespoon oil over medium heat, cook the potatoes and onion about 5 minutes, stirring occasionally. Add the green beans and garlic; cook 2 minutes longer.

Add the tomatoes, 1 cup water, bay leaf, capers, salt, crushed red pepper, cloves, and cooked meat. Bring to a boil over high heat; reduce the heat to low. Cover and simmer 45 minutes, stirring occasionally. Add the artichoke hearts; cover and simmer 15 minutes longer, or until the meat and vegetables are tender, stirring occasionally.

Meanwhile, in a 1-quart saucepan, bring 1½ cups water to a boil. Add the couscous; cover and remove from the heat. Let stand 5 minutes. Remove the bay leaf. Serve the stew over the couscous.

SAUSAGE, POTATOES, AND PEPPERS

Sweet Italian sausages can be substituted in this comforting mélange of obvious Italian origin. Serve with crusty rolls and a sprightly red wine.

Serves 4.

1 pound hot Italian sausage
1½ pounds all-purpose potatoes, peeled and cut into 1-inch
    chunks
1 large red bell pepper, seeded and cut into ¼-inch strips
1 large green bell pepper, seeded and cut into ¼-inch strips
1 large onion, sliced
½ teaspoon salt
½ cup water

In a 12-inch skillet over medium heat, cook the sausage until well browned on all sides, turning occasionally and pricking with a fork. Remove to a plate.

In the drippings remaining in the skillet over medium heat, cook the potatoes 10 minutes, stirring occasionally. Add the peppers, onion, and salt; cook 5 minutes longer.

Cut the sausage into ½-inch-thick slices. Add to the skillet with the water. Simmer 5 minutes, or until the sausages are tender, stirring occasionally.

PASTA WITH POTATOES AND SPICY SAUSAGES

Starch lovers of the world unite! This potato, pasta, and spicy sausage combo makes a perfect supper for a cold winter night.

Serves 6.

1 pound hot Italian sausages
3 cups small shell pasta
¾ pound all-purpose potatoes, peeled and diced
2 large garlic cloves, crushed
2 large tomatoes, diced
½ cup chopped parsley
¼ cup grated Parmesan cheese
½ teaspoon salt

Prick the sausages with a fork. In a 12-inch skillet over medium heat, cook the sausages until well browned on all sides, turning occasionally, about 15 minutes. Remove the sausages to paper towels to drain.

Meanwhile, in a 4-quart saucepan over high heat, bring 3 quarts salted water to a boil. Add the pasta and return to a boil. Reduce the heat to medium; simmer 10 minutes until the pasta is tender. Drain. Transfer to large bowl.

Cut the sausages into ½-inch-thick slices. In the drippings remaining in the skillet over medium heat, cook the diced potatoes until lightly browned and tender on all sides, stirring frequently. Add the garlic; cook 1 minute longer. With a slotted spoon, remove the potatoes to the bowl with the pasta. Stir in the tomatoes, parsley, Parmesan cheese, and salt; toss to mix well.

SEAFOOD POTATO GUMBO

The richness of this gumbo comes from cooking the *roux* until it is dark brown. For a more fiery afterglow, increase the amount of cayenne pepper as desired.

Serves 6.

¼ *cup vegetable oil*
1 pound all-purpose potatoes, peeled and cut into
  ½-inch cubes
2 large celery stalks, diced
1 green bell pepper, seeded and diced
1 large onion, diced
2 large garlic cloves, thinly sliced
¼ *cup all-purpose flour*
One 28-ounce can tomatoes
1 cup clam juice
1 bay leaf
1¼ teaspoons salt
⅛ *teaspoon cayenne pepper*
½ *pound medium or small shrimp, peeled and deveined*
½ *pound bay scallops*
One 12-ounce can corn, drained
One 10-ounce package frozen whole okra

In a 4-quart saucepan over medium heat, heat the oil, and in it cook the potatoes, celery, green pepper, onion, and garlic for 10 minutes, stirring occasionally. With a slotted spoon, remove the vegetables to a bowl. Into the drippings remaining in the skillet, add the flour. Cook, stirring frequently until the mixture is dark brown, 5 to 10 minutes.

Add the tomatoes with their liquid, the clam juice, bay leaf, salt, cayenne pepper, and sautéed vegetables. Bring to a boil over high heat. Reduce the heat to low; cover and simmer 25 minutes.

Add the shrimp, scallops, corn, and okra. Bring to a boil over high heat. Reduce the heat to low; simmer, uncovered, 5 minutes, o until the seafood is tender, stirring occasionally. To serve, remove the bay leaf.

POTATO CHILI

Most people don't associate chili with potatoes, but this recipe will make you an instant convert. For 3-Alarm Potato Chili, add 1 teaspoon hot red pepper sauce to the mixture.

Serves 6.

2 tablespoons vegetable oil
1 pound all-purpose potatoes, peeled and cut into
 ½-inch chunks
1 large onion, chopped
1 large green bell pepper, seeded and chopped
1 large garlic clove, chopped
2 tablespoons chili powder
One 16-ounce can tomatoes
One 16-ounce can red kidney beans, drained and rinsed
1 cup water
One 6-ounce can tomato paste
1 teaspoon salt
1 teaspoon dried oregano
¼ teaspoon crushed red pepper
¼ cup chopped coriander

In a 4-quart saucepan over medium heat, heat the oil, and in it cook the potatoes, onion, and green pepper about 5 minutes, stirring occasionally. Add the garlic and chili powder; cook 1 to 2 minutes to blend flavors, stirring frequently.

Add the tomatoes with their liquid, red kidney beans, water, tomato paste, salt, oregano, and crushed red pepper. Bring to a boil over high heat. Reduce the heat to low; cover and simmer 30 minutes, stirring occasionally.

Uncover the saucepan; simmer 10 to 15 minutes longer, or until the mixture has thickened, stirring occasionally. To serve, garnish with coriander.

CHAPTER FIVE

SIDE DISHES

Fried Potato Curls

Hash Browns

Purple Potato Chips

Potato Pudding

Peppery Potato Knishes

Stuffed Sweet Potatoes

Potato, Parsnip, and Carrot Gratin

Sweet Potato and Hazelnut Croquettes

Potato, Onion, and Apple Pie

Twice-Baked Potatoes (with variations)

Herb-Roasted Potato Fans

Sausage and Potato Stuffing

Goat Cheese and Potato Tart

Rösti (Swiss Potato Cake)

Fried Mashed Potatoes

Bourbon-Mashed Sweet Potatoes

Lemon-Oregano Roasted New Potatoes

Down-Home Mashed Potatoes (with variations)

Potato Casserole Parmigiana

Pommes Anna

Potato and Parsnip Home Fries

FRIED POTATO CURLS

Crispy, paper-thin, potato "frills" are a welcome addition to any meal, especially a roast. They can make even hamburgers look elegant.

Serves 4.

2 large baking potatoes, peeled
2 large sweet potatoes, peeled
Peanut or vegetable oil
Salt to taste

With a vegetable peeler, peel paper-thin strips from the potatoes and drop the strips into a large bowl of ice water as you work. The curls can be made ahead up to this point.

In a 12-inch deep skillet or large saucepan, heat 1 inch of the oil to 400° F. Remove the potato strips from the water; pat dry with paper towels. Drop a handful of strips into the hot oil. Fry until crisp and golden, about 2 minutes. With a slotted spoon, remove the potato strips to paper towels to drain. Repeat with the remaining potato strips. Sprinkle with salt and serve.

HASH BROWNS

Hash browns are a versatile dish that can complement eggs for breakfast, or meats and poultry at dinner.

Serves 4.

¼ cup butter or margarine
1 pound all-purpose potatoes, peeled, grated, and
*   squeezed dry*
1 large onion, diced
1 medium red or green bell pepper, seeded and diced
½ teaspoon salt
⅛ teaspoon freshly ground black pepper

In a 12-inch skillet over medium-high heat, melt the butter, and in it cook the potatoes, onion, and bell pepper about 8 to 10 minutes, gently stirring the mixture every few minutes.

Add the salt and pepper; cook until the potatoes are well browned on both sides and tender.

PURPLE POTATO CHIPS

Use a *mandoline* to slice the potatoes very thin, and when frying them, be sure to bring the oil back to 375° F. in between batches. Though the recipe calls for purple potatoes, all-purpose types could be used; sweet potatoes are another choice, but they tend to get soggy.

Serves 4.

1 pound purple potatoes, peeled
1 cup vegetable or peanut oil
2 large garlic cloves, sliced
Salt to taste

Thinly slice the potatoes. Soak the slices in a bowl of cold water 5 minutes; drain well. Pat the potatoes dry.

In a deep-fryer or heavy 2-quart saucepan, heat the oil to 375° F. Add the garlic slices; cook until golden, and remove.

Cook the potato slices in batches until crisp, about 1 to 2 minutes. With a slotted spoon, remove to paper towels to drain. Sprinkle with salt. Repeat with the remaining potatoes.

POTATO PUDDING

The grated carrots in this potato kugel, or pudding, add a touch of sweetness. Serve this delightful dish with roasted or grilled poultry or meat, and don't forget the sour cream.

Serves 6.

3 large eggs
1½ pounds all-purpose potatoes, peeled and grated
2 medium carrots, peeled and grated
2 medium scallions, sliced
2 tablespoons butter or margarine, melted
1½ teaspoons baking powder
¾ teaspoon salt
¼ teaspoon freshly ground black pepper
½ cup sour cream

Preheat the oven to 350° F. Grease a 2-quart baking dish or casserole. In a large bowl, beat the eggs. Add the potatoes, carrots, scallions, butter, baking powder, salt, and pepper, and mix to combine.

Spoon the mixture into the prepared baking dish. Bake 45 to 50 minutes, or until the pudding is lightly browned and set. Top each serving with a dollop of sour cream.

PEPPERY POTATO KNISHES

These spicy potato treats are a great way to use leftover mashed potatoes. Stuff them with chopped chicken livers for rave reviews.

Makes 12 knishes.

3 pounds all-purpose potatoes
2 tablespoons vegetable oil
1 large onion, finely chopped
2 large eggs
2 tablespoons snipped chives
2 teaspoons salt
1 teaspoon freshly ground black pepper
3 tablespoons rendered chicken fat, shortening, butter, or
  margarine

Place the unpeeled potatoes and enough water to cover in a 4-quart saucepan over high heat and bring to a boil. Reduce the heat to low; cover and simmer 25 to 30 minutes, until the potatoes are tender. Drain.

Meanwhile, in a 1-quart saucepan or small skillet over medium heat, heat the oil, and in it cook the onion until tender and very lightly browned, about 10 minutes, stirring occasionally.

Peel the potatoes when they are cool enough to handle. Place them in a large bowl and mash well. Add the cooked onion, eggs, chives, salt, and pepper; stir until well mixed.

Preheat the oven to 350° F. Grease a large jelly-roll pan. Shape ½ cup of the mixture at a time into a 3-inch oval, about 1 inch thick; place in pan. Top each knish with some chicken fat. Bake 30 minutes. Turn the knishes; bake 30 minutes longer, or until they are lightly browned. Serve warm.

STUFFED SWEET POTATOES

Don't wait for Thanksgiving to serve these. Family and friends will be thankful for them year-round.

Serves 4.

4 large sweet potatoes
4 tablespoons butter or margarine, melted
4 teaspoons light or dark brown sugar
¼ teaspoon salt

Preheat the oven to 400° F. Wash the sweet potatoes, scrubbing them well to remove any dirt or soil. With a fork, prick the sweet potatoes. Place on the oven rack; bake about 45 minutes, or until a knife inserted in the center goes in easily. Remove the potatoes from the oven.

Carefully cut off one-third of each potato lengthwise. Scoop out and remove the pulp from the potato, leaving a ¼-inch-thick shell. Scoop out all pulp from the potato tops, and discard the tops.

In a large bowl, mix well the potato pulp, butter, brown sugar, and salt. Fill the potato shells with the hot mixture, mounding it slightly. Serve immediately.

POTATO, PARSNIP, AND CARROT GRATIN

Root vegetables are not only comforting, but also incredibly nutritious. This elegant and colorful gratin is perfect with roast turkey.

Serves 6.

¾ pound all-purpose potatoes, very thinly sliced
2 medium parsnips, peeled and thinly sliced
2 large carrots, peeled and thinly sliced
1 small leek, chopped
2 large garlic cloves, crushed
1 teaspoon salt
¼ teaspoon freshly ground black pepper
One 13¾-ounce can chicken broth
½ cup grated Parmesan cheese

Preheat the oven to 400° F. Grease a 13-×9-inch baking dish. In a large bowl, toss the potatoes, parsnips, carrots, leek, garlic, salt, and pepper.

Spoon half of the vegetable mixture into the dish; pour the chicken broth over the vegetables. Sprinkle with ¼ cup of the Parmesan cheese. Top with the remaining vegetable mixture and cheese. Bake 1 hour, or until the potatoes are tender and the gratin is hot and bubbly.

SWEET POTATO AND HAZELNUT CROQUETTES

A crisp nut crust and a meltingly tender filling. What could be better? These croquettes can accompany small roast birds—pheasant, perhaps, or Cornish hens.

Serves 4.

3 tablespoons butter or margarine
1 medium onion, finely chopped
1 cup mashed sweet potatoes
1 teaspoon grated lemon peel
3/4 teaspoon salt
1/4 teaspoon freshly ground black pepper
1 large egg, separated
3/4 cup ground hazelnuts
1 tablespoon vegetable oil

In a 12-inch skillet over medium heat, heat 2 tablespoons of the butter or margarine, and in it cook the onion until tender, about 5 minutes, stirring occasionally.

In a large bowl, combine the onion mixture, mashed sweet potatoes, lemon peel, salt, pepper, egg yolk, and 1/4 cup of the hazelnuts until well blended.

In a small bowl, lightly beat the egg white. Place the remaining 1/2 cup hazelnuts in a small bowl. Shape 2 tablespoonfuls of the sweet potato mixture into a 2-inch round ball. Roll each round in the egg white, then in the hazelnuts to coat well.

In the same skillet over medium heat, heat the oil and the remaining 1 tablespoon butter; cook the sweet potato croquettes about 4 minutes, turning them once.

POTATO, ONION, AND APPLE PIE

This savory pie is modeled after a classic German country dish— *Himmel und Erd*—which translates to "sky and earth," signifying apples and potatoes. *Un*traditionally, it's topped here with a flaky pastry crust, then baked until golden.

Serves 6.

PASTRY

1¾ cups all-purpose flour
¼ teaspoon salt
¾ cup butter or margarine
¼ cup sour cream

FILLING

4 ounces bacon, diced
1½ pounds red potatoes, cut into 1-inch chunks
1 large onion, diced
3 large Golden Delicious apples, peeled, cored, and cut into
*   1-inch chunks*
¾ cup water
¼ cup chopped parsley
¼ teaspoon salt
½ cup shredded Cheddar cheese

In a large bowl, combine the flour and salt. With a pastry blender or 2 knives used scissor-fashion, cut in the butter until the mixture resembles coarse crumbs. Stir in the sour cream until the dough holds together. Turn the dough out onto a lightly floured surface, and knead it gently a few times. Cover and refrigerate until it is easy to roll out, about 2 hours.

Meanwhile, in a 12-inch skillet over medium heat, cook the bacon until lightly browned and crisp, 5 to 10 minutes, stirring occasionally. With a slotted spoon, remove the bacon to a plate.

CHAPTER FIVE

In the drippings remaining in the skillet, cook the potato chunks and onion about 10 minutes, stirring occasionally. Add the apples; cook 5 minutes longer. Add the water and bring to a boil over high heat. Reduce the heat to low and simmer, uncovered, until the potatoes and apples are tender. Stir in the parsley, salt, and bacon. Spoon the mixture into a 9-inch deep-dish pie plate or casserole. Sprinkle the mixture with Cheddar cheese.

Preheat the oven to 400° F. On a lightly floured surface, roll the pastry into a 10-inch circle. Place the pastry circle on the filling; fold the overhang under and press gently all around the pie plate to make a fluted edge. Cut a few slits in the center of the pastry to allow steam to escape.

Bake the pie about 25 minutes, or until the crust is golden and the filling is heated through.

TWICE-BAKED POTATOES

Everyone's mom has a favorite twice-baked potato recipe. Here is one you can count on, with a variety of serving suggestions.

Serves 4.

4 large baking potatoes
Vegetable oil
One 8-ounce package cream cheese, at room temperature
¼ cup minced parsley or snipped chives
1 teaspoon salt
1 teaspoon paprika
¼ teaspoon freshly ground black pepper
1 tablespoon butter or margarine, melted

Preheat the oven to 450° F. Scrub the potatoes to remove any dirt. Dry the potatoes and prick them with a fork. Rub the potato skins lightly with oil. Place the potatoes on a cookie sheet or jelly-roll pan. Bake 45 minutes, or until tender.

Cut the potatoes in half lengthwise. Scoop out the pulp from each potato half, leaving a ¼-inch-thick shell. In a large bowl, mash the potato pulp. Add the cream cheese, parsley, salt, paprika, and pepper; beat with a wire whisk or fork until light and fluffy.

With a large pastry bag fitted with a rosette tip (or with a spoon), pipe the potato mixture into the potato shells, mounding it on top. Place the potatoes on a cookie sheet. Brush the tops with the melted butter.

Bake 10 minutes, or until the potatoes are heated through and the top is lightly browned.

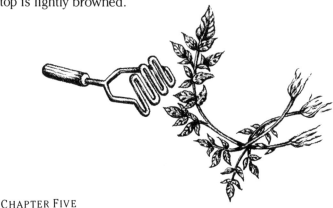

CHAPTER FIVE

FILLING VARIATIONS

Mash the potato pulp; sprinkle with salt and pepper to taste, and add:

Cottage cheese and chopped fresh herbs
Finely chopped ham and minced scallions
Minced smoked salmon and snipped chives
Refried beans, shredded Monterey Jack cheese, and chopped
    green chilies
Chopped hard-cooked eggs and chopped parsley
Chipped beef and diced red and green bell peppers
Steamed chopped mixed vegetables
Finely chopped mushrooms
Crumbled bacon
Chopped chicken livers
Condensed cream of shrimp soup
Chopped smoked chicken or turkey and minced tarragon
Drained flaked tuna and minced red onion
Chopped spinach and nutmeg

Spoon potato mixture into shells and bake.

HERB-ROASTED POTATO FANS

As these potato slices cook, they actually fan out, becoming crispy on the outside and tender in the inside.

Serves 4.

4 tablespoons butter or margarine
1 large garlic clove, minced
2 teaspoons chopped fresh thyme leaves or ½ teaspoon dried thyme
½ teaspoon salt
4 medium baking potatoes

Preheat the oven to 400° F. In a small saucepan over medium-low heat, melt the butter; stir in the garlic. Cook 1 minute; remove from the heat. Stir in the thyme and salt; set aside.

Peel the potatoes. Cut each potato crosswise into ¼-inch-thick slices, being careful not to cut all the way through. Place in a 9- × 9-inch baking pan. Brush the potatoes with the herb butter. Bake 1 hour, or until the potatoes fan out and are golden, brushing them occasionally with the herb butter in the pan.

SAUSAGE AND POTATO STUFFING

This savory mixture can be used to stuff a chicken or Cornish hen. Or, double it to stuff a turkey.

Makes 4 cups.

2 tablespoons vegetable oil
1 pound all-purpose potatoes, diced
One 12-ounce tube bulk pork sausage
4 ounces mushrooms, diced
¼ cup chopped parsley

In a 12-inch skillet over medium heat, heat the oil, and in it cook the diced potatoes for 15 minutes, or until almost tender, stirring occasionally. With a slotted spoon, remove the potatoes to a large bowl.

In the drippings remaining in the skillet over medium-high heat, cook the sausage about 10 minutes, breaking up the meat with a fork. Add the mushrooms; cook 5 minutes longer, stirring occasionally, until the sausage and mushrooms are cooked through. With a slotted spoon, remove the mixture to the bowl of potatoes. Add the parsley; toss to mix well.

Preheat the oven to 350° F. Grease a 2-quart casserole. Spoon the potato stuffing into the casserole. Cover and bake 30 to 40 minutes, or until heated through.

GOAT CHEESE AND POTATO TART

This savory tart makes an ideal side dish with roast beef or lamb. Or, serve as is for brunch.

Serves 6.

Pastry for one 9-inch pie
¾ pound all-purpose potatoes, thinly sliced
4 ounces creamy goat cheese or ricotta cheese
1 cup chicken broth
2 large scallions, sliced
¼ cup chopped fresh basil, or 2 teaspoons dried basil
1 large garlic clove, crushed
½ teaspoon salt

Preheat the oven to 425° F. On a lightly floured surface, roll the pastry into a 11-inch round. Line a 9-inch fluted tart pan with the pastry, pressing it onto the bottom and up the side of the pan; trim the edge. Prick the pastry with a fork in many places. Bake the pastry for 10 minutes.

Meanwhile, place the potatoes and enough water to cover in a 2-quart saucepan over high heat and bring to a boil. Reduce the heat to low; cover and simmer 5 to 10 minutes, or until the potatoes are just tender. Drain well.

In a large bowl, combine the potato slices, goat cheese, chicken broth, scallions, basil, garlic, and salt; toss to mix well. Spoon the mixture into the tart shell.

Cover with foil and bake 30 minutes. Remove the foil, and bake 10 minutes longer, or until the crust is browned and the filling is set. Cut into wedges.

RÖSTI
[SWISS POTATO CAKE]

The Swiss have their own version of hash browns. The shredded potatoes cook into a cake with a crispy crust and a tender, oniony interior that goes wonderfully with scrambled or poached eggs.

Serves 6.

4 slices bacon, diced
2 pounds all-purpose potatoes, peeled
¼ cup sliced scallions or well-washed leeks
¾ teaspoon salt
¼ teaspoon freshly ground black pepper
2 tablespoons butter or margarine

In a 10-inch skillet over medium heat, fry the bacon until just cooked, stirring frequently. Remove to a bowl.

Shred the potatoes; do not rinse. Pat dry with paper towels. Toss in a bowl with the bacon, scallions, salt, and pepper. Add the butter to the skillet with the bacon drippings; heat over medium heat. Add shredded potatoes. Cook until the bottom is golden brown and crusty, about 5 minutes, shaking the pan occasionally. Reduce the heat to low and cook 5 minutes longer. Cover the skillet with a flat plate; invert the skillet, turning the potato "cake" out onto the plate. Carefully slide the potato cake back into the skillet; increase the heat to medium; repeat the cooking method, adding more butter if necessary.

To serve, slide the potato cake onto a heated serving platter; cut into wedges.

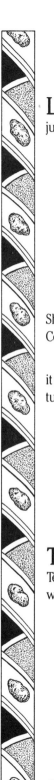

Fried Mashed Potatoes

Leftovers *can* be fun—and delicious. If you don't have chives on hand, just use minced shallots or red onions in this recipe.

Serves 4.

2 cups leftover mashed potatoes
¼ cup snipped chives
½ cup dried seasoned bread crumbs
1 tablespoon vegetable oil
1 tablespoon butter or margarine

In a medium bowl, combine the mashed potatoes and the chives. Shape the mixture into four 3½-inch round patties about ½ inch thick. Coat the patties with the seasoned bread crumbs.

In a 12-inch skillet over medium heat, heat the oil and butter, and in it cook the patties until they are golden on both sides, about 5 minutes, turning once.

Bourbon-Mashed Sweet Potatoes

These yummy bourbon-mashed sweet potatoes can perk up any meal. Teetotalers may substitute freshly squeezed orange juice for the whiskey.

Serves 4 to 6.

3 pounds sweet potatoes
¼ cup butter or margarine, melted
2 tablespoons bourbon
¾ teaspoon salt
¼ teaspoon freshly ground black pepper
¼ cup chopped toasted pecans

Place the sweet potatoes and enough water to cover in a 3-quart saucepan over high heat and bring to a boil. Reduce the heat; cover and simmer 25 minutes, or until the potatoes are tender. Drain.

Peel the potatoes. Place in a large bowl and mash. Stir in the butter, bourbon, salt, and pepper until they are well mixed. Sprinkle with toasted pecans.

LEMON-OREGANO ROASTED NEW POTATOES

The refreshing flavors of lemon and oregano bring out the best in this side dish, which is a perfect accompaniment to broiled lamb chops or a roast leg of lamb.

Serves 4.

2 pounds new potatoes, cut into 1-inch chunks
¼ cup olive oil
3 tablespoons chopped fresh oregano or 1 tablespoon dried
  oregano
2 tablespoons lemon juice
½ teaspoon salt
¼ teaspoon freshly ground black pepper
2 teaspoons grated lemon peel

Preheat the oven to 450° F. In a 13- × 9-inch baking pan, toss the potatoes with the olive oil, oregano, lemon juice, salt, and pepper.

Roast the potatoes for 30 minutes, stirring occasionally, until lightly browned and tender.

To serve, toss the potatoes with the grated lemon peel.

DOWN-HOME
MASHED POTATOES

Here is a classic recipe for mashed potatoes. As a variation, try browning the butter first to give them a distinctive, nutty flavor.

Serves 6.

4 large baking potatoes, peeled
¼ cup heavy cream
¼ cup butter or margarine
2 teaspoons chopped parsley
1½ teaspoons salt
¼ teaspoon freshly ground black pepper

Place the potatoes and enough water to cover in a 4-quart saucepan over high heat and bring to a boil. Reduce the heat to low; cover and simmer 30 minutes, or until the potatoes are tender. Drain. Return the potatoes to the saucepan and shake them over heat to remove any excess moisture.

Into a large bowl, press the hot potatoes through a ricer, or mash well. In a small saucepan, heat the cream and butter until warm; stir into the mashed potatoes along with the parsley, salt, and pepper. Serve immediately.

SERVING SUGGESTIONS

Try stirring into the mashed potatoes:

> Any chopped fresh herbs—chives, basil, thyme, marjoram, or sage
>
> Chopped pitted olives—black or pimiento-stuffed
>
> Shredded cheese—Cheddar, Muenster, Monterey Jack, Blue, Parmesan, or Brie
>
> Cooked and crumbled bacon or ham bits
>
> Buttered bread crumbs—rye or whole wheat bread
>
> Seeds—caraway, sesame, or sunflower
>
> Onion salt with sour cream and cream cheese
>
> Green chilies or chopped jalapeño peppers
>
> Chopped onions—cooked white or red onions, scallions, or leeks
>
> Peppers—chopped pimientos, roasted red peppers, diced red, green, or yellow bell peppers
>
> Chopped pickles or pickle relish
>
> Sautéed green cabbage
>
> Sour cream or cream cheese
>
> Chopped salami, pepperoni, or crumbled cooked sausage

For guilt-free mashed potatoes: omit the butter and cream; stir in low-fat yogurt and/or low-fat ricotta cheese

POTATO CASSEROLE PARMIGIANA

Here is a recipe for potato purists. Potatoes, Parmesan cheese, broth, and a few flavorings are baked together, with marvelous results.

Serves 4.

1½ cups water
1 vegetable bouillon cube or envelope
6 small baking potatoes, peeled and sliced
2 large scallions, sliced
1 teaspoon salt
¼ teaspoon freshly ground black pepper
½ cup grated Parmesan cheese

Preheat the oven to 400° F. In an ovenproof 12-inch skillet over high heat, bring the water and bouillon cube to a boil. Stir in the potatoes, scallions, salt, pepper, and ¼ cup of the Parmesan cheese; toss to mix well. Bake 25 minutes, or until the potatoes are tender. Remove from the oven.

Increase the heat to broil. Sprinkle the remaining Parmesan cheese over the top of the potatoes, and broil about 3 minutes longer, or until they are golden.

POMMES ANNA

Pommes Anna is a classic French recipe that relies upon only two ingredients, plus seasoning. Sliced potatoes are layered, generously brushed with butter, and baked until crisp. It sounds simple, and *is*. The result is resoundingly good.

Serves 3.

1 pound baking potatoes, peeled
4 tablespoons butter or margarine, melted
Salt and freshly ground black pepper to taste

Cut the potatoes into very thin slices, about 1/16 inch thick. (You can use a food processor with the slicer blade attached or a *mandoline.*)

Brush an 8-inch cast-iron skillet or pie plate with 1 tablespoon butter. Arrange one-third of the potato slices in a circular fashion, slightly overlapping them, over the bottom. Sprinkle lightly with salt and pepper. Brush with 1 tablespoon of the butter. Repeat the layers 2 more times, ending with butter.

Cover the potatoes with foil; weigh them down with a flat heavy lid, cake pan, or pie plate. Bake 30 minutes. Remove the weight and foil. Bake 15 to 20 minutes longer, or until the potatoes are browned and crisp on top.*

To serve, carefully invert the potatoes onto a serving platter. Cut into wedges.

*As an easy variation, create Potatoes au Gratin simply by sprinkling on grated Cheddar cheese and placing in the broiler for approximately 1 minute, or until the cheese melts.

POTATO AND PARSNIP
HOME FRIES

Use a cast-iron skillet here for browning the potatoes and parsnips, to make them nice and crispy. You can also recycle "last night's" leftover baked potatoes for this dish, in which case you will only be boiling the parsnips in the first step below.

Serves 6.

1 pound all-purpose potatoes
1 pound parsnips
¼ cup butter or margarine
1 large onion, diced
1½ teaspoons salt
1 teaspoon paprika
½ teaspoon freshly ground black pepper

In a 2-quart saucepan, bring 2 inches of water to a boil over high heat. Meanwhile, peel the potatoes and parsnips; cut them into ½-inch pieces, and add them to the boiling water. Boil 10 minutes, or until tender. Drain well.

Meanwhile, in a 12-inch skillet over medium heat, melt the butter, and in it cook the onion about 5 minutes, stirring occasionally.

Add the potatoes and parsnips, salt, paprika, and pepper to the skillet, and cook 5 to 10 minutes longer over medium-high heat, stirring frequently, until the vegetables are golden brown.

CHAPTER SIX

BREADS, ROLLS, AND MUFFINS

Spiced Potato-Honey Biscuits

Potato-Corn Mini Muffins

Potato Pumpernickel Bread

Golden Potato Harvest Braids

Potato and Ale Peasant Bread

"Potted" Sweet Potato Tea Bread

Maple-Glazed Sweet Potato Doughnuts

Sweet Potato Dinner Rolls

Potato Buttermilk Biscuits

Potato Parsley Drop Scones

Herbed Potato Bread

Potato Focaccia

Sweet Potato-Banana Quick Bread

Sweet Potato-Orange Muffins

Spiced Sweet Potato Pancakes

Sweet Potato Date-Nut Bread

SPICED POTATO-HONEY BISCUITS

Serve these biscuits warm from the oven with a touch of your favorite fruit preserves. Sweet butter goes nicely, too.

Makes 2 dozen biscuits.

2½ cups all-purpose flour
4 teaspoons baking powder
¾ teaspoon ground ginger
½ teaspoon salt
⅓ cup vegetable shortening
1 cup mashed sweet potatoes
¾ cup milk
2 tablespoons honey

Preheat the oven to 450° F. Grease 2 large cookie sheets. In a large bowl, combine the flour, baking powder, ginger, and salt. With a pastry blender or two knives used scissor-fashion, cut in the shortening until the mixture resembles coarse crumbs.

In a medium bowl, stir the mashed sweet potatoes, milk, and honey. Stir into the flour mixture. On a lightly floured surface, knead the dough about 30 seconds. Pat the dough into a ¾-inch-thick piece.

With a 2-inch round cookie cutter, cut all the dough, including the scraps, into rounds. Place the rounds on the prepared cookie sheets about 2 inches apart. Bake 12 to 15 minutes, or until the dough is puffed and golden. Remove to a wire rack to cool slightly. Serve warm.

POTATO-CORN MINI MUFFINS

These mini muffins are a natural with barbecued chicken or ribs. If you have some, try them topped with pepper jelly.

Makes 2 dozen muffins.

4 strips bacon, diced
1¼ cups all-purpose flour
¾ cup yellow cornmeal
¼ cup granulated sugar
2 teaspoons baking powder
1 teaspoon salt
1 cup mashed potatoes
½ cup milk
¼ cup vegetable oil
1 large egg

Preheat the oven to 400° F. Grease twenty-four 1½-inch gem muffin pans. In a 10-inch skillet over medium-high heat, cook the bacon until browned and crisp, stirring occasionally. Remove to paper towels to drain. When cool enough to handle, crumble.

In a large bowl, combine the flour, cornmeal, sugar, baking powder, and salt. In a medium bowl, stir the mashed potatoes, milk, oil, egg, and crumbled bacon.

Stir the potato mixture into the flour mixture until just blended. Spoon the mixture into the prepared pans to fill almost to the top. Bake 15 to 20 minutes, until the muffins are lightly browned and puffed. Remove to a wire rack to cool slightly. Serve warm.

POTATO PUMPERNICKEL BREAD

Here is a chewy, peasant bread, with a hint of molasses and caraway. Shape the dough into small rounds, bake, and serve as deliciously different dinner rolls.

Makes 2 loaves.

2½ cups rye flour
2 packages active dry yeast
1 tablespoon caraway seeds
2 teaspoons salt
5 cups all-purpose flour
2 cups milk
1 cup mashed potatoes
½ cup light molasses
¼ cup vegetable shortening

In a large bowl, combine the rye flour, yeast, caraway seeds, salt, and 2 cups of the all-purpose flour. In a 1-quart saucepan over low heat, heat the milk until warm (120° to 130° F.). With a mixer at low speed, gradually beat the warm milk into the dry ingredients until blended. Add the potatoes, molasses, and shortening. Increase speed to medium; beat 2 minutes. Beat in ½ cup all-purpose flour to make a thick batter. With a wooden spoon, stir in 2 cups all-purpose flour to make a soft dough.

Turn the dough out onto a floured work surface and knead until it is smooth and elastic, working in the remaining ½ cup all-purpose flour while kneading. Shape the dough into a ball and place in a large greased bowl, turning the dough over to grease the top. Cover with a towel and let rise in a warm place until doubled, about 1 hour.

Grease 2 large cookie sheets. Punch down the dough and cut in half, and shape each half into a ball. Place each ball on a cookie sheet. Cover and let rise in a warm place until doubled, about 1 hour.

Preheat the oven to 375° F. Bake the rounds about 25 minutes, or until they sound hollow when lightly tapped. Remove to wire racks to cool.

GOLDEN POTATO HARVEST BRAIDS

Soft-textured and moist, these braids get their color and irresistible flavor from sweet potatoes.

Makes 2 braids.

2 packages active dry yeast
1 tablespoon granulated sugar
1 teaspoon salt
8 cups bread flour or all-purpose flour
1 cup milk
1 cup water
2 tablespoons butter or margarine
3 large eggs
1 cup mashed sweet potatoes
2 tablespoons kosher salt

In a large bowl, combine the yeast, sugar, salt, and 2 cups of the flour. In a 1-quart saucepan over low heat, heat the milk, water, and butter until warm (120° to 130° F.). Stir into the flour mixture until blended. Stir in 2 of the eggs and the sweet potatoes until well blended. Gradually stir in 5½ cups flour until the mixture makes a soft dough.

On a floured surface, knead the dough 5 minutes, or until smooth and elastic, kneading in about ½ cup flour. Shape the dough into a ball and place in a large greased bowl, turning the dough over to grease the top. Cover with a towel and let rise in a warm place until doubled, about 1 hour.

Grease 2 large cookie sheets. Punch down the dough and divide it in half. Working with one half at a time, cut into 3 equal pieces. With

your hands, roll each piece into a 12-inch-long rope. Place ropes side by side on cookie sheets. Start braiding from the middle of the ropes. Shape the braid into a ring; pinch the ends to seal. Repeat with the remaining dough. Cover and let rise in a warm place until doubled, about 45 minutes.

Preheat the oven to 400° F. In a small cup, beat the remaining egg. Brush the braids with the beaten egg; sprinkle with the kosher salt. Bake the braids about 25 minutes, or until the bread sounds hollow when lightly tapped. Remove to wire racks to cool.

POTATO AND ALE PEASANT BREAD

The little bit of ale in this bread goes a long way and keeps good company with the potatoes in the dough. Serve with pork, country ribs, or a simple bean dish.

Makes 1 loaf.

1½ cups all-purpose flour
1 cup mashed potatoes
1 large egg
¼ cup grated Parmesan cheese
1½ teaspoons baking powder
1½ teaspoons salt
1 large garlic clove, crushed
¼ cup ale or beer

Preheat the oven to 375° F. In a large bowl, combine the flour, potatoes, egg, Parmesan cheese, baking powder, salt, and garlic; stir in the ale.

Using your hands, knead the mixture until it forms a round loaf. Place on a small greased cookie sheet. With a knife, cut slashes in the top of the dough. Bake 45 minutes, or until golden and the loaf sounds hollow when tapped with your fingers. Remove to a wire rack to cool.

"Potted" Sweet Potato Tea Bread

A great year-round gift idea for the spud lover, this sweet potato tea bread can be presented in a flower pot. Embellish it with a garden shovel, hoe, and seed packets. If you don't have a terra-cotta flower pot on hand, use a 9- × 5-inch loaf pan.

Makes 1 loaf.

2½ cups all-purpose flour
1 cup chopped pecans
½ cup granulated sugar
4 teaspoons baking powder
¾ teaspoon ground allspice
1 cup mashed sweet potatoes
1 large egg
½ cup milk
½ cup orange marmalade, plus additional for brushing, if
  desired
¼ cup butter or margarine, melted
½ cup dark raisins

Preheat the oven to 350° F. Soak a new, clean, 6-inch-wide (top end) terra-cotta flower pot in cold water for 10 minutes; drain. Line the pot with aluminum foil; grease the foil. Cut a circle of foil to fit the bottom of the pot; press it into the pot and grease.

In a large bowl, stir the flour, pecans, sugar, baking powder, and allspice to mix well. In a medium bowl with a wire whisk or fork, beat the sweet potatoes, egg, milk, orange marmalade, butter, and raisins; stir into the flour mixture just until blended. Spoon the batter into the prepared flower pot. Bake 1½ hours, or until a toothpick inserted in the center comes out clean. Cover the loaf with foil during the last 15 minutes of baking if the top becomes too brown. Remove to a wire rack to cool.

Remove the bread from the flower pot; peel off the foil. If you like, brush the top with orange marmalade.

Maple-Glazed
Sweet Potato Doughnuts

Sweet potato doughnuts are bread-like in texture. Serve them with morning coffee, or with brunch.

Makes 2 dozen doughnuts.

3½ cups all-purpose flour
4 teaspoons baking powder
1 tablespoon ground allspice
1¼ cups granulated sugar
2 large eggs
2 tablespoons butter or margarine, melted
1 cup mashed sweet potatoes
½ cup milk
1 teaspoon maple extract
6 cups vegetable oil for frying
½ teaspoon ground cinnamon
¼ cup maple syrup

In a large bowl, stir the flour, baking powder, allspice, and 1 cup sugar. In a small bowl, combine the eggs, butter, sweet potatoes, milk, and maple extract.

Add the sweet potato mixture to the flour mixture until the dough is just combined. Cover the dough; chill 1 hour.

Working with half of the dough at a time, roll the dough out on a floured work surface with a floured rolling pin to a ½-inch thickness. Cut the dough with a floured 2½-inch doughnut cutter. Repeat with the remaining dough.

In a deep, heavy 12-inch skillet, heat the oil over medium-high heat until a deep-fry thermometer reaches 375° F. Fry the doughnuts in batches until golden, about 2 to 3 minutes, turning once. Remove to paper towels to drain.

In a small bowl, combine the cinnamon and ¼ cup sugar. While they are still warm, lightly brush the doughnuts with the maple syrup and sprinkle with the cinnamon sugar.

SWEET POTATO DINNER ROLLS

Most people wouldn't think of making their own dinner rolls from scratch. But you won't find sweet potato rolls in the market, so try this recipe. And what could be nicer than the incomparable aroma of bread baking wafting through your house. These are fabulous served warm with sweet butter.

Makes 15 rolls.

2 packages active dry yeast
2 teaspoons salt
5½ cups all-purpose flour
1¼ cups milk
¼ cup butter or margarine
1½ cups mashed sweet potatoes
1 large egg
1 egg white
1 tablespoon sesame seeds

In a large bowl, combine the yeast, salt, and 2 cups of the flour. In a 1-quart saucepan over low heat, heat the milk and butter until warm (120° to 130° F.), stirring frequently.

With a mixer on low speed, gradually beat the liquid into the dry ingredients just until blended; beat in the sweet potatoes and the egg. On medium speed, beat 2 minutes, occasionally scraping the bowl. Beat in 1 cup flour to make a thick batter; continue beating 2 minutes, scraping the bowl often. Stir in enough additional flour (about 1½ cups) to make a soft dough.

On a floured surface, knead the dough 10 minutes until smooth and elastic; knead in the remaining 1 cup of flour. Shape the dough into a ball and place in a large greased bowl, turning the dough over to grease the top. Cover with a towel and let rise in a warm place until doubled, about 1 hour.

Punch down the dough; turn out onto a lightly floured surface. Cut into 15 pieces. Shape into balls. Place in a greased 13- × 9-inch baking pan. Cover and let rise until doubled, about 30 minutes.

CHAPTER SIX

Preheat the oven to 400° F. Brush the rolls with the egg white; sprinkle them with sesame seeds. Bake 20 minutes, or until the rolls sound hollow when tapped. Remove to a wire rack to cool.

POTATO BUTTERMILK BISCUITS

Buttermilk can be made by adding 1 teaspoon lemon juice to 1 cup of milk. In most cases, it adds a tangy flavor, but here it imparts an appealing mellowness.

Makes 12 biscuits.

2 cups all-purpose flour
2 teaspoons baking powder
½ teaspoon baking soda
½ teaspoon salt
¼ cup butter or margarine, melted
1 cup mashed potatoes
¾ cup buttermilk

Preheat the oven to 425° F. In a large bowl, combine the flour, baking powder, baking soda, and salt. With a pastry blender or 2 knives used scissor-fashion, cut in the butter until the mixture resembles coarse crumbs.

Stir in the mashed potatoes and buttermilk until the mixture forms a mass. Shape into a ball.

On a lightly-floured surface, knead the dough about 30 seconds. Pat the dough into a ¾-inch-thick piece. With a 2½-inch round cookie cutter, cut 12 circles, including all the scraps.

Arrange the biscuits, 1 inch apart, on a cookie sheet. Bake 10 to 12 minutes, or until golden and puffed. Remove to wire racks to cool slightly. Serve warm, or cool to serve later.

POTATO PARSLEY DROP SCONES

Scones are now available in almost any flavor imaginable. These offer the chance to use up leftover mashed or baked potatoes in an interesting and savory way. Serve with a big pot of stew or soup.

Makes 10 scones.

2¼ cups all-purpose flour
¼ cup granulated sugar
⅔ cup packed light brown sugar
2 teaspoons baking powder
½ teaspoon baking soda
½ cup butter or margarine, softened slightly
2 large eggs
¾ cup mashed potatoes
½ cup sour cream
¼ cup chopped parsley
¼ cup milk

Preheat the oven to 425° F. In a large bowl, combine the flour, both sugars, the baking powder, and baking soda. With a pastry blender or 2 knives used scissor-fashion, cut in the butter until the mixture resembles coarse crumbs.

Stir in 1 of the eggs, the mashed potatoes, sour cream, parsley, and milk until the mixture holds together.

Drop ⅓ cup of the mixture at a time onto a large greased cookie sheet and brush the batter with the remaining egg, beaten lightly. Bake 15 minutes, or until the scones are golden. Remove to a wire rack to cool slightly. Serve warm or at room temperature.

HERBED POTATO BREAD

Potatoes add a savory richness to this fresh-baked yeast bread, which is enhanced by a touch of thyme and parsley.

Makes 2 loaves.

¼ cup granulated sugar
1 package active dry yeast
1½ teaspoons salt
6 to 6½ cups all-purpose flour
1½ cups milk
2 large eggs
1 cup mashed potatoes
2 tablespoons chopped parsley
2 teaspoons dried thyme

In a large bowl, combine the sugar, yeast, salt, and 1½ cups of the flour. In a small saucepan over low heat, warm the milk (120° to 130° F.). Stir the warm milk into the dry ingredients until blended. Stir in the eggs, mashed potatoes, parsley, and thyme until well blended. Gradually add 4½ cups of the flour until the mixture makes a soft dough.

On a floured surface, knead the dough 5 minutes, or until smooth and elastic, kneading in about ½ cup of the remaining flour. Shape the dough into a ball and place in a large greased bowl, turning the dough over to grease the top. Cover with a towel and let rise in a warm place until doubled, about 1 hour.

Punch down the dough and divide it in half. Shape the halves into round loaves. Place the loaves on a large baking sheet, seam side down. Cover with a towel and let rise in a warm place until doubled, about 45 minutes.

Preheat the oven to 375° F. Place the baking sheet on the center rack of the oven and bake 30 minutes, or until the breads are browned and sound hollow when tapped with your fingers. Remove the breads to a wire rack to cool.

POTATO FOCACCIA

Focaccia is a rustic Italian hearth bread, usually baked in a brick oven. This recipe uses potatoes in the dough as well as on top of it. Serve it with a hearty soup, stew, or warm salad.

Serves 10.

> 1 package active dry yeast
> 4 cups all-purpose flour
> 3 teaspoons salt
> 1 cup milk
> ¾ cup mashed potatoes
> ¼ cup olive oil
> 1 pound all-purpose potatoes, peeled and diced
> 2 large garlic cloves, minced
> ¾ cup oil-packed sun-dried tomatoes, cut into strips
> 1 tablespoon chopped fresh thyme, basil, or rosemary
> ¼ teaspoon freshly ground black pepper
> ¼ cup crumbled goat cheese

Preheat the oven to 400°. In a large bowl, combine the yeast, 2 cups of the flour, and 2 teaspoons salt. In a 1-quart saucepan over low heat, warm the milk (120° to 130° F.). With the mixer on low speed, beat the milk into the dry ingredients until just blended. Add ½ cup of the flour, the mashed potatoes, and 1 tablespoon of the olive oil; beat 2 minutes. With a spoon, stir in 1½ cups flour to make a soft dough.

Turn the dough out onto a lightly floured surface and knead until it is smooth and elastic, about 5 minutes, gradually kneading in more flour if necessary.

Grease a jelly-roll pan. Pat the dough into the prepared pan. Cover and let rise in a warm place until doubled, about 1 hour.

Meanwhile, in a 12-inch skillet over medium heat, add the remaining 3 tablespoons olive oil, and in it cook the diced potatoes about 8 minutes, stirring occasionally. Add the garlic; cook 2 minutes longer, or until the potatoes are tender. Stir in the sun-dried tomatoes, thyme, pepper, and 1 teaspoon salt.

Evenly spoon the potato mixture over the dough in the pan; sprinkle with the goat cheese. Bake on the lower rack of the oven for 20 minutes, or until the crust is golden.

SWEET POTATO-
BANANA QUICK BREAD

Ever wonder what to do with a leftover, overripe banana? Stick it in the freezer, and when there are enough, thaw and mash them. They're great to use in making banana bread.

Makes 2 large or 4 small loaves.

1 cup butter or margarine, softened
2 cups granulated sugar
4 large eggs
2½ cups all-purpose flour
2 teaspoons baking powder
½ teaspoon salt
1 cup mashed sweet potatoes
1 cup mashed ripe bananas
1 teaspoon vanilla extract

Preheat the oven to 350° F. Grease two 8- × 4-inch or four 5- × 3-inch loaf pans. In a large bowl with an electric mixer at medium speed, beat the butter and sugar until well blended. Add the eggs; beat until smooth.

In a small bowl, combine the flour, baking powder, and salt. Stir the flour mixture into the egg mixture. Stir in the sweet potatoes, bananas, and vanilla until just blended. Spoon the mixture into the prepared pans. Bake large loaves for 1 hour, smaller loaves 50 minutes, or until a toothpick inserted in the center comes out clean. Remove to a wire rack to cool in the pans.

SWEET POTATO-ORANGE MUFFINS

Studded with raisins and spiked with orange flavor, these muffins should be served warm with sweet butter.

Makes 12 muffins.

1 large sweet potato
1½ cups all-purpose flour
1 cup packed light brown sugar
1 teaspoon baking powder
¾ teaspoon ground allspice
½ teaspoon baking soda
¼ teaspoon salt
2 large eggs
¼ cup vegetable oil
¼ cup orange juice
1 cup golden raisins
1 tablespoon grated orange peel

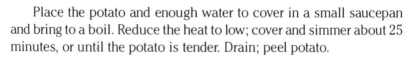

Place the potato and enough water to cover in a small saucepan and bring to a boil. Reduce the heat to low; cover and simmer about 25 minutes, or until the potato is tender. Drain; peel potato.

Preheat the oven to 400° F. Grease twelve 2½-inch muffin tins. In a large bowl, combine the flour, brown sugar, baking powder, allspice, baking soda, and salt. In a medium bowl, combine the eggs, oil, orange juice, and mashed sweet potato; stir into the dry ingredients until just mixed. Quickly fold in the raisins and orange peel.

Spoon the batter into the prepared muffin tins. Bake 18 to 20 minutes, or until a toothpick inserted in center comes out clean. Remove the muffins to wire racks to cool slightly. Serve warm.

CHAPTER SIX

SPICED SWEET POTATO PANCAKES

These pancakes are a spicy Saturday morning treat. Drop fresh or frozen blueberries into the batter, and serve, blueberried or not, with warm maple syrup.

Makes ten 3-inch pancakes.

1¼ cups all-purpose flour
3 tablespoons light brown sugar
1¼ teaspoons baking powder
½ teaspoon ground cinnamon
¾ cup milk
½ cup mashed sweet potatoes
1 large egg
1 teaspoon vanilla extract
1 teaspoon grated lemon peel
2 tablespoons butter or margarine
Warm maple syrup

In a large bowl, mix the flour, brown sugar, baking powder, and cinnamon. Add the milk, sweet potatoes, egg, vanilla, and grated lemon peel; stir just until flour is moistened.

Heat a griddle or 12-inch skillet over medium heat; melt 1 tablespoon of the butter. Pour the batter by scant ¼-cupfuls onto the hot griddle. Cook until the tops are bubbly and the edges are dry. With a pancake turner, turn the pancakes. Cook until the undersides are golden. Keep warm.

Repeat with remaining butter and batter. Serve the pancakes with warm maple syrup.

Sweet Potato Date-Nut Bread

Date-nut bread makes an appealing and tasty gift. In addition to the method used in this recipe, these loaves can also be baked in four 5¾-×4½-inch loaf pans for 20 to 25 minutes. Spread liberally with softened cream cheese for a rich, delicious treat, or top with marmalade.

Makes 2 loaves.

2½ cups all-purpose flour
⅔ cup packed dark brown sugar
1 teaspoon baking powder
1 teaspoon baking soda
1½ cups mashed sweet potatoes
1 large egg
½ cup milk
¼ cup butter or margarine, melted
1 teaspoon vanilla extract
1 cup chopped pitted dates
1 cup chopped walnuts
1 tablespoon grated lemon peel

Preheat the oven to 350° F. Grease two 8-×4-inch loaf pans. In a large bowl, combine the flour, brown sugar, baking powder, and baking soda. In a medium bowl, combine the sweet potatoes, egg, milk, melted butter, and vanilla.

Stir the sweet potato mixture into the flour mixture until just blended. Quickly stir in the dates, walnuts, and grated lemon peel. Spoon the mixture into the prepared pans.

Bake 45 to 50 minutes, or until a toothpick inserted in the center comes out clean. Remove the loaves to wire racks to cool.

CHAPTER SEVEN

DESSERTS

Sweet Potato Gingerbread

Sweet Potato Praline Pie

Sweet Potato Spice Cookies

Mocha-Frosted Potato Cake

Gingered Sweet Potato Cheesecake

Sweet Potato Bundt Cake

Sweet Potato and Peach Tart

Brandied Sweet Potato Pudding

Potato Streusel Coffee Cake

Potato Marzipan

Sweet Potato Bread Pudding

Sweet Potato Fudge Drops

Sweet Potatoes and Bananas in Rum

Sweet Potato Gingerbread

Traditional gingerbread is not made with sweet potatoes, but they lend a certain crumble to the crumb of this cake that's truly special.

Serves 12.

2 cups all-purpose flour
1 cup mashed sweet potatoes
1 large egg
¾ cup molasses
½ cup sugar
½ cup milk
½ cup butter or margarine, softened
1 teaspoon baking soda
1 teaspoon ground ginger
½ teaspoon ground cinnamon
¼ teaspoon ground nutmeg
1 cup whipped cream
1 tablespoon grated orange peel

Preheat the oven to 325° F. Grease a 9-×9-inch baking pan. In a large bowl, combine the flour, sweet potatoes, egg, molasses, sugar, milk, butter, baking soda, ginger, and cinnamon. With an electric mixer on low speed, beat the ingredients until well blended.

Increase the speed to medium; beat 2 minutes longer. Spoon the batter into the pan. Bake 1 hour, or until a toothpick inserted in the center comes out clean. Remove to a wire rack to cool, or serve warm. Serve with whipped cream sprinkled with grated orange peel.

SWEET POTATO PRALINE PIE

Classic elements of a Southern kitchen—brown sugar, pecans, and sweet potatoes—come together in this casual dessert.

Serves 8.

Pastry for one 9-inch pie

FILLING

2 cups mashed sweet potatoes (or one 24-ounce can sweet potatoes, drained and mashed)
½ cup sugar
½ cup packed light brown sugar
2 tablespoons butter or margarine, softened
3 large eggs
1 cup half-and-half
1 tablespoon grated orange peel
1½ teaspoons ground allspice
1 teaspoon maple extract

PRALINE TOPPING

¾ cup chopped pecans
¾ cup packed light brown sugar
3 tablespoons butter or margarine, melted
¼ teaspoon maple extract

On a lightly floured surface, roll the pastry into a 15-inch round. Fit into a 9-inch pie plate. Trim the edge, leaving a 1-inch overhang. Turn the dough under. Flute the edge or make a decorative edging.

Preheat the oven to 400° F. In a large bowl with an electric mixer at medium speed, beat the sweet potatoes, granulated sugar, brown sugar, butter, eggs, half-and-half, orange peel, allspice, and maple extract to blend thoroughly. Pour the mixture into the prepared crust. Bake 45 minutes, or until a knife inserted in the center comes out clean. Remove to a wire rack to cool.

To prepare the topping: Preheat the broiler. In a medium bowl, combine all the topping ingredients. Spoon the topping over the pie. Broil 2 to 3 minutes, or until the topping is glazed.

SWEET POTATO SPICE COOKIES

Sugar and spice and everything nice—including molasses, cinnamon, ginger, and *especially* sweet potatoes—are the tasty ingredients in these cookie "gems." Despite the fact that they're healthier than the average cookie, confirmed dessert lovers will still adore them.

Makes 2½ dozen cookies.

2½ *cups all-purpose flour*
1 cup mashed sweet potatoes
⅓ cup butter or margarine, softened
¼ cup light molasses
¼ cup maple syrup
2 teaspoons baking soda
1 teaspoon ground cinnamon
1 large teaspoon ground ginger
1 egg
¾ cup sugar

In a large bowl with an electric mixer at low speed, combine the flour, sweet potatoes, butter, molasses, maple syrup, baking soda, cinnamon, ginger, egg, and ½ cup of the sugar.

Preheat the oven to 350° F. Place the remaining ¼ cup sugar in a small bowl. Shape the dough, 2 tablespoons at a time, into balls; roll the balls in the sugar. Place the balls on large ungreased cookie sheets, about 1½ inches apart. Press each ball to ½-inch thickness. Bake 15 minutes, or until browned. Remove from the oven and cool on a rack.

MOCHA-FROSTED POTATO CAKE

At the turn of the century, American cooks added potatoes to a cake to compensate for a lack of flour, which was often difficult to obtain. Plus, potatoes rendered a moist cake, one that lasted for several days.

Serves 12.

1 cup butter or margarine, softened
1½ cups packed light brown sugar
3 large eggs
1 cup mashed sweet potatoes
2 cups all-purpose flour
¼ cup cocoa powder
1 tablespoon instant coffee powder
2 teaspoons ground cinnamon
1 teaspoon baking soda
1 teaspoon baking powder
1 cup milk
2 cups toasted chopped almonds

CREAMY MOCHA FROSTING

1 cup butter or margarine, softened
3 cups confectioners' sugar
⅓ cup semisweet chocolate chips, melted and cooled slightly
1 tablespoon instant coffee powder

Preheat the oven to 350° F. Grease and flour two 8-inch round cake pans. In a large bowl with an electric mixer on high speed, cream the butter and brown sugar until light and fluffy. Add the eggs and the sweet potatoes and mix until well blended.

In a small bowl, combine the flour, cocoa, coffee powder, cinnamon, baking soda, and baking powder until well mixed. With the mixer on low speed, gradually add the flour mixture and milk to the sweet potato mixture until well blended. Increase the speed to medium; beat 1 minute. Stir in 1 cup of the almonds. Spoon the mixture into the prepared pans.

Bake 40 minutes, or until a toothpick inserted in the center comes out clean. Remove to wire racks; cool 10 minutes. Remove the cakes from the pans and cool completely.

To make the frosting: In a large bowl with the mixer on low speed, beat the butter or margarine until smooth. Add the confectioners' sugar, chocolate, and coffee powder; beat until the frosting is smooth and spreadable.

Place 1 cake layer on a serving plate. Spread with some of the mocha frosting recipe. Top with the remaining cake layer; frost the top and sides.

Press the remaining 1 cup chopped almonds onto the sides.

GINGERED SWEET POTATO CHEESECAKE

There are all kinds of cheesecakes, but this one—with sweet potatoes, cream cheese, sour cream, and spices—is unique.

Serves 16.

1 cup crushed gingersnaps
½ cup ground walnuts
¼ cup butter or margarine, melted
Three 8-ounce packages cream cheese, softened
1½ cups packed light brown sugar
2 cups mashed sweet potatoes (or one 24-ounce can sweet
*   potatoes, drained and mashed)*
3 large eggs
1 cup sour cream
2 teaspoons ground ginger
1½ teaspoons vanilla extract
1 teaspoon ground cinnamon
Chopped crystallized ginger for garnish

In a 9-inch springform pan, combine the gingersnaps, walnuts, and melted butter; press into the bottom of the pan.

Preheat the oven to 350° F. In a large bowl with an electric mixer on medium speed, beat the cream cheese and brown sugar until light and fluffy. With the mixer on low speed, beat in the sweet potatoes, eggs, sour cream, ginger, vanilla, and cinnamon until smooth.

Pour the filling into the prepared crust. Bake 1 hour, or until the cheesecake is set. Remove from the oven. Cool the cake on a wire rack completely. Refrigerate until ready to serve.

To serve, garnish the top of the cheesecake with chopped crystallized ginger.

SWEET POTATO BUNDT CAKE

Here is a moist, spiced cake, thanks to the sweet potatoes. Serve with tea or for dessert with a generous helping of homemade applesauce.

Serves 12.

1½ cups butter or margarine, softened
1¼ cups granulated sugar
1 cup packed dark brown sugar
4 large eggs
1½ cups mashed sweet potatoes
2 teaspoons vanilla extract
3 cups all-purpose flour
2 teaspoons baking soda
2 teaspoons ground cinnamon
2 teaspoons ground nutmeg
½ teaspoon salt
1 cup chopped pecans
Confectioners' sugar

Preheat the oven to 350° F. Grease a 10-cup Bundt pan. In a large bowl with an electric mixer on medium speed, beat the butter, granulated sugar, and brown sugar until smooth and creamy.

Add the eggs, sweet potatoes, and vanilla; beat until smooth. In a small bowl, stir together the flour, baking soda, cinnamon, nutmeg, and salt. Add to the egg mixture. With the mixer on low speed, beat 2 minutes until well blended, occasionally scraping the bowl with a rubber spatula. Stir in the pecans.

Spoon the batter into the prepared pan. Bake 1 hour, or until a toothpick inserted into the center of the cake comes out clean. Remove to a wire rack; cool 10 minutes. Remove the cake from the pan. Cool completely.

To serve, dust the cake lightly with confectioners' sugar.

SWEET POTATO AND PEACH TART

Peach lovers will thrill to this simple, fresh dessert. By all means, opt for fresh peaches in summertime to intensify the flavor. Add a dollop of cream to top it off.

Serves 8.

Pastry for one 9-inch pie

2 cups mashed sweet potatoes (or one 24-ounce can sweet potatoes, drained and mashed)
1 large egg
⅓ cup packed light brown sugar
½ teaspoon ground ginger
½ cup peach preserves
One 16-ounce can sliced peaches, drained*

On a lightly floured surface, roll the pastry into an 11-inch circle; fit into a 9-inch fluted tart pan with a removable bottom, pressing gently but firmly against the sides to adhere. Roll the rolling pin over the top of the pan to trim off the excess dough.

Preheat the oven to 375° F. In a large bowl with an electric mixer on low speed, beat the sweet potatoes, egg, brown sugar, ginger, and ¼ cup of the peach preserves until well blended. Spoon the mixture into the prepared tart shell. (If you are using fresh peaches, blanch them in boiling water for 30 seconds to loosen their skins.) Arrange the peach slices in concentric circles on top of the filling.

Bake 45 minutes, or until the crust is golden and the potato mixture is cooked. Remove to a wire rack to cool.

In a small saucepan over low heat, heat the remaining ¼ cup peach preserves. Brush the peaches on the top of the tart with the preserves.

*In season, substitute 3 large fresh peaches, peeled, pitted, and sliced.

BRANDIED SWEET POTATO PUDDING

Although this pudding is usually served for dessert, it's also delicious served with roast ham or pork.

Serves 6.

3 pounds sweet potatoes
2 large eggs
½ cup packed light brown sugar
¼ cup milk
¼ cup brandy or cognac
¼ cup butter or margarine, melted
½ teaspoon salt
1 cup chopped pecans

Place the sweet potatoes and enough water to cover in a 3-quart saucepan over high heat and bring to a boil. Reduce heat to low; cover and simmer 30 minutes, or until tender. Drain.

When cool enough to handle, peel the potatoes. Mash them well, or press through a ricer. In a large bowl, combine the sweet potatoes, eggs, brown sugar, milk, brandy, butter, and salt until well mixed.

Preheat the oven to 375° F. Grease a 2-quart casserole. Spoon the sweet potato mixture into the casserole. Sprinkle with the chopped pecans. Bake 30 minutes, or until the mixture is heated through. Serve warm, or refrigerate to serve chilled later.

Potato Streusel Coffee Cake

Based on a Moravian sugar cake, this yeast-risen coffee cake updates a classic. While the mashed potatoes do add moistness, yeast cakes, in general, do not keep as long as quick breads. Serve in large pieces!

Serves 12.

½ cup milk
¼ cup butter or margarine
2 packages active dry yeast
½ cup granulated sugar
¾ cup mashed potatoes
2 large eggs
¼ teaspoon salt
3 cups all-purpose flour

STREUSEL TOPPING

¾ cup all-purpose flour
¼ cup packed light or dark brown sugar
⅓ cup chopped walnuts
½ teaspoon ground cinnamon
⅓ cup butter or margarine, softened

In a 1-quart saucepan over low heat, heat the milk and butter until warm (120° to 130° F). Stir in the yeast; set aside until mixture is bubbly, about 10 minutes.

In a large bowl, combine the sugar, mashed potatoes, eggs, salt, and 2 cups of the flour. With an electric mixer on low speed, beat in the yeast mixture for about 2 minutes. Stir in the remaining 1 cup flour. The dough will be sticky.

Place the dough in a large greased bowl, turning it over to grease the top. Cover and let rise in a warm place until doubled, about 1 hour.

Grease a 13- × 9-inch baking pan. Spoon the dough into the pan and spread it to cover the pan evenly. Cover and let rise 1 hour.

Meanwhile, prepare the topping: In a medium bowl, combine the flour, brown sugar, walnuts, and cinnamon. Cut in the butter until the mixture forms coarse crumbs.

Preheat the oven to 375° F. Sprinkle the topping evenly over the dough. Bake 15 to 20 minutes, or until the top is golden. Remove to a wire rack to cool slightly. Cut into squares; serve warm.

Potato Marzipan

This is a variation on classic marzipan, which is made with ground almonds and sugar. Shape this interesting combination into diminutive fruits or vegetables and serve as sweets with after-dinner coffee.

Makes 2 cups.

½ cup mashed potatoes
½ teaspoon almond extract
4½ cups confectioners' sugar

In a small bowl with an electric mixer on low speed, beat the potatoes and the almond extract until smooth. Gradually beat in the confectioners' sugar to make a stiff dough.

Shape the potato marzipan into potatoes, apples, pears, bananas, strawberries, oranges, or other fruits or vegetables; let dry on a tray. Brush with food color to simulate the various fruits, or roll in cocoa to resemble potatoes. Store in a covered container in a cool place for up to 1 week.

SWEET POTATO
BREAD PUDDING

True comfort food—this homey bread pudding has layers of cinnamon-raisin bread, mashed sweet potatoes, and creamy custard. A Sunday-night supper dessert, if there ever was one.

Serves 8.

2¼ cups milk
2 large eggs
½ cup packed light brown sugar
½ teaspoon ground nutmeg
¼ cup butter or margarine, softened
12 slices cinnamon-raisin bread
1 cup mashed sweet potatoes
Confectioners' sugar

Preheat the oven to 325° F. Butter an 11-×9-inch baking dish. In a large bowl, combine the milk, eggs, brown sugar, and nutmeg. Set the mixture aside.

Spread butter on one side of each bread slice. Arrange 6 slices of the bread, buttered side up, in the prepared baking dish. Spoon the mashed sweet potatoes onto the bread slices, spreading evenly. Top with the remaining bread slices. Pour the egg mixture over the bread.

Bake 1 hour, or until the mixture is set and top is lightly browned. To serve, sprinkle with confectioners' sugar. Serve warm.

CHAPTER SEVEN

SWEET POTATO FUDGE DROPS

These fudgy-nut cookies make a tempting treat for a child's lunch box or a family outing. (The sweet potatoes just add fiber—you can't really taste them!)

Makes 6 dozen cookies.

½ cup butter or margarine, softened
1 cup packed dark brown sugar
1 large egg
1 cup mashed sweet potatoes
Four 1-ounce squares semisweet chocolate, melted
1 teaspoon vanilla extract
2 cups all-purpose flour
1 teaspoon baking powder
1 teaspoon ground cinnamon
½ teaspoon baking soda
½ cup walnut pieces

Preheat the oven to 375° F. Grease several large cookie sheets. In a large bowl with an electric mixer on high speed, beat the butter and brown sugar until light and fluffy. Add the egg, sweet potatoes, chocolate, and vanilla; beat until the ingredients are well combined.

Into a medium bowl, combine the flour, baking powder, cinnamon, and baking soda. Add the dry ingredients to the sweet potato mixture. Beat until just blended.

Drop the mixture by heaping tablespoonfuls, spaced 1½ inches apart, onto the cookie sheets. Press a walnut piece into the center of each cookie. Bake 10 minutes. Remove to wire racks to cool.

SWEET POTATOES AND BANANAS IN RUM

Top each serving of this melt-in-your-mouth dessert with vanilla ice cream. Its flavorful sauce helps take off winter's chill.

Serves 2.

2 small sweet potatoes, peeled
3 tablespoons butter or margarine
2 tablespoons dark brown sugar
1 large banana, peeled and sliced
2 tablespoons dark rum
¼ teaspoon ground cinnamon
¼ cup finely chopped pecans

Cut the sweet potatoes lengthwise in half; cut the halves crosswise into ¼-inch-thick slices. In a 10-inch skillet over medium heat, melt the butter, and cook in it the sweet potato slices until tender and lightly browned, about 4 to 5 minutes, stirring occasionally.

Stir in the brown sugar until it is dissolved. Add the banana slices; cook 1 to 2 minutes until heated through. Add the rum and cinnamon; cook until the mixture is thickened slightly. Divide among dessert plates and garnish with the pecans.

INDEX